Tory Christie

CHICKEN SCRATCH BOOKS
WWW.CHICKENSCRATCHBOOKS.COM

Text Copyright © 2023 by Tory Christie
Illustrations Copyright © 2023 by Connie Resch

All rights reserved. No part of this publication may be reproduced, distributed or transmitted in any form or by any means, including photocopying, recording, or other electronic or mechanical methods, without the prior written permission of the publisher, except in the case of brief quotations embodied in critical reviews and certain other noncommercial uses permitted by copyright law. For permission requests, write to the publisher, addressed "Attention: Permissions Coordinator," at the address below.

Chicken Scratch Books
PO Box 104
Wisdom, MT 59761
www.chickenscratchbooks.com

Publisher's Note: This is a work of fiction. Names, characters, places, and incidents are a product of the author's imagination. Locales and public names are sometimes used for atmospheric purposes. Any resemblance to actual people, living or dead, or to businesses, companies, events, institutions, or locales is completely coincidental.

Ordering Information: Special discounts are available on quantity purchases by corporations, associations, and others. For details, contact the publisher at the address above.

First Chicken Scratch Books Printing, 2022
ISBN 978-1-953743-26-8 (paperback)
ISBN 978-1-953743-27-5 (ebook)

Printed in the United States of America

*For Brooke and Claire,
whose gentle spirits inspired this story, and
Julianna for being my first reader*

Part 1:
CHOOSE YOUR SUBJECT

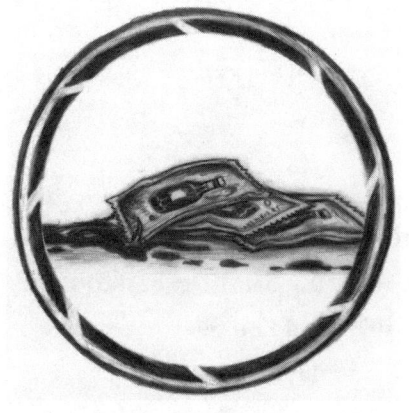

"A camera tells a story without words."

—McGill's Guide to Wildlife Photography

Chapter One

Ten is the best age; it's all downhill after that. At least that's what my Aunt Doreen told me. The best year of my life would be over in exactly one month and twenty-one days.

I trudged to the bus stop on the last day of school, feeling as crummy as you'd expect a girl to feel knowing her days of fun and youth were over. That was when I saw Honey Brooks for the first time, studying her feet, eating potato chips for breakfast.

Her family had just moved to Limbo Creek Court—six houses on the outskirts of town. And the thing is, living here is like a slow-motion scene in a movie, where seconds stretch into minutes and days last for weeks. It was already 1970, but our black and white TV got only one staticky station. The crackly voice on our transistor radio chattered about farm news, in case you wanted to know the price of a hog. And the population sign at the edge of town hadn't changed since 1948.

We hardly ever saw anyone new, which is why I was so surprised to see Honey Brooks.

One of my brothers leaned in and whispered, "Ask her, Celie."

So, I did all the talking while the boys tossed pebbles across the road and pretended they weren't listening. "Where did you come from?" I asked, inching closer.

"Omaha," Honey said, scraping a red cowboy boot through the gravel. The boots were so huge, I wasn't sure how she kept them on.

"How old are you?"

"Ten," she said, "... almost." She seemed real small for her age. And skinny. Her dress hung from her like she was a clothes line.

I stood taller and said, "I'm eleven ... almost."

Honey Brooks glanced up and smiled with the most perfect white teeth I ever saw. I ran my tongue across my chipped bottom tooth.

"Why'd your mom make you go to the last day of a new school?" I asked.

"She didn't." Honey's eyes darted around. "I want to go."

"Why?"

"Because of the crayons. *Lemon Yellow* is my

favorite." She looked down and tapped her boots together.

"Huh?"

"And the pencils." Honey hugged her rusty Snoopy lunchbox.

"What do you mean?"

She shrugged. "Everybody gets rid of that stuff on the last day of school."

"But at the end of the year, pencils are stubby and broke," I said. "They're no good."

"They're good enough." She clutched her lunchbox tighter and whispered, "Sometimes, I even get water colors."

I didn't know what to say. Aunt Doreen always told me to change the subject when things got awkward, so I said, "My name is Celie. Cecilia Blue LaRue."

"Blue," Honey breathed. "I wish I was named after a color."

"Not a color. Blue is for Blue Heron. And LaRue is because I am the great-great-great grandchild of a French-Canadian fur trader—" I began. And a Norwegian, a Swede, and a whole lot of other things. Which sometimes makes me feel like a whole lot of nothing. But I couldn't explain all that because something slithered over my shoulder.

I screamed—just a little—and snatched the garter snake before it slid down my shirt.

Honey's mouth hung open with half-chewed

potato chips.

Laughter bubbled up behind me and I spun around to face the boys. It was just a trick—the kind you get used to when you have four brothers. They got my fiercest glare.

Once they knew I wasn't scared of a teeny-tiny snake, they tried to get it back—hands grabbing at me from all directions. But I shoved that critter in my backpack as the bus squealed to a stop in front of us.

I forgot about the snake as soon as I stepped on the bus. It must have snuggled in the bottom of my backpack, first lulled by the bouncy bus and later by Miss Snedsrud's droning on and on and on about verbs and adjectives and reading over the summer.

I may have forgotten about the snake, but I did not forget about Honey Brooks. I wondered why she really came to the last day of a new school. It couldn't possibly be for the abandoned crayons. I wondered if Honey liked to climb trees. I wondered if we would be friends—even if she was only a third grader.

As the only girl in the fourth grade, my options were limited. In fact, I only had one friend, Junior Greyhawk. And that hadn't been going too great lately.

Junior watched the window like someone waiting for the ice cream truck on a hot day. He wadded pea-sized bits of paper and lined them up on his desk. He pulled out a straw and stuck one of the pea-sized bits into his mouth, getting it all soggy.

A fly bounced against the window. It buzzed until it plinked against the glass, then slowed, dazed for a second, before buzzing and plinking against the glass again. Buzzing and plinking and buzzing and plinking.

I felt for that fly, trapped, waiting for someone to set it free.

Splat. A spitball hit the window and the fly buzzed off. As the gooey wad of wet paper slid down the glass, something outside caught my eye.

Beyond the playing fields, a bush trembled. Rustling leaves moved along the edge of the woods, down County Road 2, and kept moving west. Goosebumps prickled my arms as I thought about some wild animal wandering down from Wampus Woods.

Splat! Another spitball hit the window.

"Junior Greyhawk!" Miss Snedsrud slammed *Math for the Modern World* onto her desk. I had a sickly, fluttery feeling in my stomach thinking about Junior getting yelled at again.

Fortunately for him, the bell rang. Chairs scraped against the floor as kids shrieked and rushed away from classrooms, toward buses that would take them to farms or trailer parks, or cabins up north.

I sped toward the exit, like a dog after a squirrel.

"Celie, wait!" Junior shouted.

I spun around to tell him about Honey Brooks. But as Junior grabbed my arm, my backpack full of last-day-of-school junk slipped from my shoulders. Papers and broken crayons scattered across the floor. I tried to grab for my ruler and left-handed scissors, but a swarm of kids kicked them down the hall. My stuff mingled with a forest of paper scraps and desk litter, skidding across the floor and out the front door of Pearl A. Pickleman Elementary.

That's when I remembered the snake.

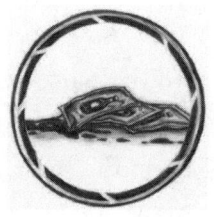

Chapter Two

The snake slithered out of my backpack, wiggling toward Freda Geagle, our school secretary. She propped open the doors as kids rushed by. I got all prickly with goosebumps again, thinking that snake might slither up her bare legs and under her dress.

But she focused on her chocolate bar and Junior grabbed the snake. He cradled it like it was a baby kitten, then slipped it into his pocket. Super quick, saving me—and Miss Geagle—from disaster.

"Thanks!" I shouted at Junior as I rushed after a drawing I made a week before. I was so proud of that drawing: me squeezed between my brothers and our parents. Mom was eight months pregnant, but I drew her holding a tiny pink bundle.

I really needed a sister.

I reached for that drawing just as it slid out the

door under an army of sneakers.

While kids ran to catch buses, I ran out the door. I scrambled after pencils and worksheets. I grabbed at papers, not knowing if they were mine or a second grader's spelling test. I reached again for the trampled drawing, but the wind picked it up and blew it into a puddle.

"Sorry, Celie!" Junior grabbed his pink banana seat bicycle from the rack and followed me down the sidewalk. "I just wanted to know if you'll be in summer school."

"Summer school?" I shook the muck off my picture. "What about all our adventures? Climbing trees? Fishing for sunnies? Biking to Ellie Mae's Ice Cream Emporium for butter brickle cones?"

Junior gripped his handlebars and glanced at my artwork. "If you took the photography class with me, you could take real pictures."

"But to take pictures you have to stand so . . . still." I knew all about photography since Dad was into cameras. I wasn't sure I had the patience for it. And to tell the truth, a class seemed kinda boring. But I didn't want to hurt Junior's feelings.

"Fine." He turned his handlebars west and jammed his foot onto a pedal. "It's only for gifted students anyway."

"What?" I felt as if I had just been punched in the gut.

When Junior moved here the second week of school, I played on the monkey bars with him when none of the other fourth graders would. He was with me the day I chipped my bottom tooth. He was my closest friend. But Junior had been snooty lately and I wasn't sure why.

Feeling even crummier than I had that morning, I turned to go, but my bus was rumbling down County Road 2 without me. Warm tears stung my eyes as I looked from the bus to my ruined artwork to Junior, pedaling away.

Honey Brooks walked out of school and stared at the empty bus loop. Grasping her rusty Snoopy lunchbox, she said in a hoarse whisper, "I don't know the way home." She quickly looked down, her crooked blonde bangs covering her eyes.

She was more like a stray cat than a third grader and I just knew she wouldn't survive without my help.

Chapter Three

Aunt Doreen said that ten was the perfect age. Young enough to get a kid's meal at the Tastee Freeze and old enough to walk to town on my own. So, I figured we could walk home—it was only two miles to our street in the middle of nowhere.

"Come on," I said. "We'll walk home together."

We headed down County Road 2. I tried to chit-chat because Aunt Doreen said that's how you get to know someone. It's how you make friends.

I talked about the spring wheat coming up in the field to the south. I talked about the trees to the north and how it was awful hot for the first week of June.

Honey didn't say much. I figured we were getting along just fine.

I chit-chatted all the way to Pitzel's Loaf & Bait, a mile out of town. The tiny store was mostly for tourists—the last stop for hunters and anglers before they headed north. Pitzel's stood at the corner of County Road 2 and Cameron Bridge Road, a one-lane dirt path into the woods.

The door jingled as we walked in.

Gerty Bigheart was perched on a stool behind the cash register. She glanced up from her newspaper. "Look what the cat dragged in!"

Honey flinched and inched away from the counter.

Gerty was short and round. But her permed brown hair was shaped like a beehive, which made her seem taller. Gerty's huge glasses slid down, almost to the tip of her nose. She caught them just in time.

"Hi Gerty," I said. "We're just browsing."

"Enjoy the selection," Gerty said, which was kind of funny. There wasn't much to choose from unless you really liked fishing bobbers and bug spray and single rolls of toilet paper.

The store smelled like stale coffee and warm baloney. The baloney smell was from the hotdogs on the front counter, spinning around and around on rollers, all glossy and greasy. The stinky smell was supposed to get you to buy a hotdog before you left the store. Then you could smother it in ketchup from a pile of packets in an old bait bucket next to the day-old donuts. But late in the day, those hotdogs got all dry and crinkly. Eating one wouldn't be a good idea.

"Got any money?" I asked Honey, as we checked out the candy stand squeezed between all the fishing tackle.

"Just my lucky quarter," she said.

"That's no good." I fingered a note in my pocket along with the ten-dollar bill I had saved from my last birthday. "You can't spend a lucky quarter."

Honey stopped and backed up when she saw Gerty's cousin. Midge Pitzel looked a lot like Gerty except she was nearly six feet tall and wore her hair extra short. And she was real old—about forty. She bought her jeans from the Farmer's Fleet and wore a bowling shirt every day of the year. Kids that didn't know better were afraid of her. Midge ran the bait shop in the back of the store, while Gerty handled the money. It worked out real well. Gerty loved to talk. Midge preferred perch over people.

I waved at Midge. But she glared in the other direction.

Toward Rat Hurley. He sauntered down an aisle with those long skinny legs and knocked a box of cough drops onto the floor. Rat was older—at least thirteen—and the meanest kid in town. Rat wasn't his real name, but even his mother called him Rat.

I grabbed Honey's hand and pulled her back behind the candy stand. We peeked around the Hershey bars as Rat stopped to study the fishing jigs. Honey's hand was clammy and I felt the sweat trickle down my back. I held my breath and worried about how we were going to escape without Rat seeing us.

The door jingled. And there was Junior, strolling through the door with that carefree bounce that always boosted my spirits. Count on good-old Junior Greyhawk to save the day! I tried to flag him over before Rat saw him, but Junior was moving straight toward Rat. I had to do something.

"Junior!" I shouted. "We're taking the shortcut to my house, want to come?" I was pretty impressed by my quick thinking. Junior loved the wooded trail that we called the shortcut. And Rat wouldn't want to pester all three of us.

Rat looked up at Junior. Then over at Honey and I holding hands. He smirked. I shivered and squeezed Honey's hand tighter.

Junior looked from Rat to us, and shrugged. "Nah."

I tried again. "We're going to run through the sprinkler!"

Junior shrugged. "Girls are boring," he said.

I jerked back in shock—like I had been petting a friendly dog and suddenly a bee stung my hand.

Junior shuffled over to Rat, who gave him a friendly punch on the shoulder.

My chest tightened. They flicked through packages of tackle as if they were best friends. Then Junior glanced over at me with a Rat-like smirk.

My face flushed hot and stingy. I forced myself to breathe. Then I squeezed Honey's hand tighter and dragged her toward the door.

Gerty called after us. "Come back when you can stay longer!"

Honey and I stepped onto County Road 2, as a big brown car zipped toward us, dust flying and gravel crunching under its tires. I hopped out of the way, pulling Honey into the grass. But the car slowed and turned onto Cameron Bridge Road.

As the dust from the car settled, Junior walked out of Pitzel's Loaf & Bait and over to the pop machine. He kicked that pop machine as Rat stepped out of the store, brushing his hand across his buzzed white hair. The sun glinted off Rat's giant belt buckle, as he swaggered toward Junior.

"We better go," I said, still stinging from Junior's betrayal. But Honey stood still, staring at the boys.

Junior looked my way and then pulled my snake out of his pocket. He showed Rat, who took the poor little snake and dangled it like a wet noodle. Rat gave the snake back to Junior. Then Junior dangled the snake too! I got an icky feeling in the pit of my stomach—Junior loved snakes.

Rat made a show of pulling a load of ketchup packets out of his pocket—the ketchup for the glossy and greasy hotdogs that no one wanted to eat.

No one, that is, except Junior's uncle, Sheriff Greyhawk. The sheriff pulled his pickup truck into the parking lot and climbed out. He waved at Junior, shook his head at Rat, and rushed into the store. Rat shoved some packets into Junior's hands and they scrambled around the pickup.

"What are they doing?" Honey whispered.

"Shhhhhh..." I tugged her sleeve. "We should really go."

But Honey wouldn't budge.

Junior and Rat stuck a pile of ketchup packets behind each tire. Then they dashed over by the pop machine to watch.

A minute later, Sheriff Greyhawk toddled out of the store, balancing a hot dog on top of a giant cup of coffee.

More gravel crunched along County Road 2. Freda Geagle's green slug bug sailed toward us. I knew exactly what was going to happen, so I pulled Honey into the ditch to hide.

Sheriff Greyhawk climbed into his truck, as Miss Geagle pulled in on his right. Her door popped open and her feet and legs poked out first. She scooted her butt on the seat, cheek by cheek. Holding the steering wheel with one hand and the door frame with the other, she heaved herself out of the car.

Miss Geagle paused to untwist her dress. It was a pretty dress with flowers and a white collar. But the sheriff started his engine and backed up his truck. And as the tires rolled over the packets, ketchup squirted like blood in a horror movie. Miss Geagle wailed.

Junior and Rat laughed and ran for their bikes.

Chapter Four

I didn't want to get blamed for that ketchup, so I tugged Honey down Cameron Bridge Road. We ran until the road curved.

Once we were safe, we slowed down.

Cameron Bridge Road started out as gravel, but someone must have given up because the gravel ran out just past Pitzel's Loaf & Bait. The dirt road twisted and turned along Limbo Creek. Old logging roads and horse trails branched off and wandered all through Wampus Woods. A person could get lost if they weren't careful.

Cameron Bridge Road was quiet. The trees closed in; the dirt road got narrower, shadier.

"The bridge is off limits," I told Honey. "The older boys hang out there. They jump off the bridge into Limbo Creek. Aunt Doreen said it's dangerous. Except

I don't know if she was talking about the jumping or the boys."

Honey stared down Cameron Bridge Road. She cradled the Snoopy lunchbox the way Mom cradled that pink bundle in my blue-ribbon picture—the picture that was now all muddy and crumpled.

I pointed to some metal gates overgrown with sumac and vines. "Before you get to the bridge, you pass Blessed Sacrament Cemetery. That's off limits, too . . . unless you're dead."

I paused. Thoughts of Junior squeezed into my head. That judgy-wudgy look he gave me in Pitzel's was burned onto my brain. My eyes started to water, so I pushed that image right back out and kept talking.

"Just before Cameron Bridge is the trail to Cat-Scratch Clyde's. He has a wolf. And he digs through the dumpster next to Pitzel's Loaf & Bait. And he never talks. You can't trust people who never talk."

I looked at Honey. "That just slipped out," I said.

Honey shrugged, so I chit-chatted away.

"Once you cross the bridge there's a resort. Frogtown. All the cabins are tipped over. Just piles of lumber. Well, except Cabin Six, which is only half-tipped over. It's haunted. And if you make it past Frogtown you're deep into Wampus Woods. It's filled with wild dogs and bears."

When we reached Cameron Bridge, I stopped. Not because I was afraid or anything. I just figured it was time to go home. Besides, the mosquitos were getting thick. I turned and headed back toward Pitzel's Loaf & Bait.

Honey followed along, twirling in circles with her Snoopy lunchbox—which I imagined was full of broken crayons and stubby pencils. She was like a ballerina chasing the mosquitos away, but she stopped suddenly and stood still in the middle of the road facing back toward the bridge.

"What is it?" I asked.

She pointed.

From below the iron truss bridge, a man climbed up the bank and onto the road. He strolled toward us.

The first thing I noticed was the bare feet at the bottom of his skinny legs, sticking out from his rolled-up overalls. Those scrawny legs were like poles that held up his huge body and broad shoulders. He kind of reminded me of a stop sign. Cat-Scratch Clyde.

A furry animal on a leash trailed after him. My heart skipped a beat, thinking about his wolf. But when Clyde was closer, I could see that it was a dog. Not just any dog, though. A big dog. It was probably part wolf.

The dog sniffed the air and rushed ahead of Clyde. I froze. Aunt Doreen had told me that running from dogs just made them chase you. But she said the same thing about boys. I wasn't sure if I could trust her judgment.

The dog barked wildly. Clyde held the leash tight and braced his legs. But it was a *real* big dog. Clyde skidded along the gravel like he was on a dog sled gliding through snow.

"Darwin!" Clyde shouted as the dog bolted at us, his leash thrashing along behind him.

Honey dropped her lunchbox and darted into the woods. I figured the woods weren't as scary as a rabid dog, so I ran after Honey. My hair slapped my face as I whipped around. I slipped, scraping my bare knee on the gravel.

Branches smacked my legs and we crunched through the pine needles and maple leaves. Crows cawed angrily above us.

"Darwin! Darwin!" Clyde's shouts faded. But Darwin's barks didn't. So, I kept running as fast as I could.

I saw flashes of Honey's red-and-white dress ahead. She whipped through the brush, kicking up last fall's rotting leaves in her wake. One of her red cowboy boots flew into the air with the fluttering leaves.

Honey disappeared down the bank of Limbo Creek. I tumbled down after her, my shirt catching on a twig. Sticks and pine needles scraped away the skin on my stomach as I slid down to the edge of the water. I landed in the mud with my left shoe in Honey's face.

Blood trickled from Honey's mouth, all over those perfectly white teeth. That red and white dress was hiked up, her flowered underwear peeking out. I wanted to tell her that in fourth grade, she'd have to get smart and wear shorts beneath her dress. But I didn't have time. I scrambled to sit up.

We huddled together and stared up at the growling dog.

Chapter Five

The dog hovered at the top of the bank, sniffing the air. The fur behind its neck stood up and muscles quivered under its thick coat. But I was more afraid of what was standing behind that killer dog. How did such an old man run that fast? Clyde stared at us. His cheeks were sunk in and grey. Wrinkles appeared from behind his whiskers like roads on a map, spreading in every direction.

We didn't move. My heart clanged like the bell at Fish Lake Lutheran before Sunday service.

Clyde tugged at Darwin's leash. There was a flash in Clyde's green eyes. "Something's got him jumpy." He glanced around the woods, up into the tree branches, and then across Limbo Creek. "That's why he's on a leash."

He looked back at Honey, then scrounged in his

pocket and pulled out a big red hankie. He knelt toward her, and she leaned back as if Cat-Scratch Clyde was going to reach out and grab her. Or bite her with those long yellow teeth.

"Your lip's bleeding," he said, tossing the hankie to Honey.

She shuddered and dabbed her lip.

He stepped back and looked everywhere but at us, swallowing a few times, patting Darwin's head. Then he gave a quick nod and turned to go. But Darwin pulled and whined and acted like he wanted to play, when only a minute before, he wanted to eat us. Darwin sniffed the air and whined some more. Clyde gave the leash a strong tug and they walked back through the woods.

Honey wasn't breathing hard at all. She must've been used to running.

A bruise showed beneath her sweaty bangs and the blood ran down the side of her mouth. "Did I do all that?"

"It's no big deal." She stared across the creek, still sopping up blood with Clyde's hankie.

I turned to look across the creek, too. A lopsided green cabin, its windows boarded up, hid behind the birch and pine.

Frogtown.

I figured that was Cabin Six, the last cabin of the resort that once lined the creek. The other cabins were piles of rotting wood.

We sat on that muddy bank and stared into the woods on the other side of the creek. Something moved behind the fluttering leaves. Something whitish and ghostlike. But then it was gone. I shivered.

"That was the color of *Moonbeams*," Honey whispered.

"Or ghosts," I whispered back. I tried to stand up. My arms sunk into the mud. My feet shot out straight as if I were on skis and I plopped back onto the bank. When I finally stood, Honey still stared at the cabin.

"Let's go," I whispered, my heart pounding as I searched the leafy bank for wild dogs or bears.

Or ghosts.

Chapter Six

We quietly crisscrossed through the trees. I glanced back to make sure no wild dogs or bears followed. Honey kicked up the damp leaves, searching for her missing boot.

"Will your mom be mad you lost a boot?" I asked.

"I can't tell her." She didn't cry but her eyes were glossy.

"What will she do to you?" I asked. She rubbed her forehead and looked real pale. "Don't worry. We'll find it."

"It's *Brick Red*," Honey said.

I wondered about Honey's mother and wanted to ask. But in the short time since we left school, I figured out something. Aunt Doreen wasn't always right. Chit-chat wasn't the best way to make friends. So, I started asking questions.

"What about your dad?" I asked.

Honey's voice was nearly a whisper. "He's not home."

"Do you have any brothers or sisters?" I wanted to know all about her.

Honey shook her head.

"Do you have any pets?" I asked.

Honey nodded, peering into a small bush.

"A dog? A cat?" I watched her closely as she kicked more leaves up from the trail with her bare foot.

Honey nodded again.

"Which one?"

"A cat," she said.

"What's its name?"

"Nice Kitty."

"That's not a good name."

Honey shrugged. "Mother says giving it a real name makes you too attached."

I was about to ask if Honey had a real name, but stopped myself just in time. "We don't have pets," I said, because chit-chat seemed safer than questions right now. "Mom says that pets never grow up. She'd rather have babies." I told Honey we would have a new baby soon. I talked about how I cleaned my room real nice so my parents might put the crib next to my bed. They weren't so sure that was a good idea.

"There!" Honey shouted.

She rushed over to the *Brick Red* boot standing on

a pile of pine needles, as if it were waiting for her. She looked inside, probably to make sure there were no snakes, tried to scrape the mud off her bare foot, and then pulled it on. She looked at me and smiled.

We made it out of the trees and back up onto Cameron Bridge Road and my heart beat more regular. Honey picked up the Snoopy lunchbox and brushed it off.

Walking alongside Honey, I wondered about her. She *was* small and skinny. But she could run fast and she didn't cry about the bruise or the cut lip or the missing boot. She was tough. And she let me talk as much as I wanted.

I didn't need Junior or his photography class.

Honey Brooks would be the perfect person to join me on a summer adventure.

Chapter Seven

On Limbo Creek Court, Honey Brooks and I stood next to the tallest cottonwood. "It's too bad you're in third grade," I said.

"Why?" asked Honey.

"There hasn't been a girl my age since Brenda Louise Teasley moved away on picture day in the first grade." I always wondered if that was my fault—with the grape juice and pink dress. "Do you want to come in?" I blurted before I could think too much about the Brenda Louise incident.

I figured if I couldn't show Mom my blue-ribbon artwork at least I could show off Honey Brooks.

Honey glanced down the street to her house.

"We might have snacks," I added.

Honey perked up. "I like snacks." She followed me around the side of the house.

My brothers, Luke and Mark, ran through the sprinkler. Jack knelt next to his upside-down ten-speed, away from the sprinkles. He gripped a wrench in one hand and spun the back wheel with the other.

Honey and I stood near the sprinkler until the mud washed away, leaving us clean but soaked from the waist down.

I climbed the back steps and squeaked open the screen door.

The smell of warm gooey chocolate chip cookies smacked my nose. It was just like Mom to make cookies on the last day of school. I rushed into the kitchen with Honey—and stopped dead.

Mom leaned into the counter with oven mitts on her hands. She wiped her limp hair away from her forehead. Matthew slid a cookie onto a paper plate.

Mom was baking with *Matthew*.

Baking was *our* special thing together! Mom and me. She could take the boys fishing or to the movies, but not baking! Baking was the only thing we did without my brothers getting in the way.

I didn't need this on top of Junior acting so snooty today. I tried to keep my bottom lip from trembling.

Mom didn't notice.

"Who's this?" She gave Honey a big smile. Mom used to smile a lot, but lately, she was so tired she sometimes forgot.

I took a deep breath and steadied my lip. "Mom,

this is Honey Brooks."

Honey backed up, trying to blend in with the orange flowers on the wallpaper—which wasn't working too good.

"Hi, Honey." Mom glanced down at Honey's too-big clothes, but she did it so quick you could barely notice.

We stood with stiff smiles for a bit too long, Honey's eyes darting around the room like she wanted to escape. Mom opened her mouth to say something, but the screen door crashed open.

Honey flinched as the rest of my brothers rushed into the house.

"Mom! Mom! Mom!" Their shouts bounced across the linoleum, along with the water that splashed in behind them. They shoved me to the side.

"Mom!" Jack blew out a big breath and held up his greasy hands. "They keep splashing my bike!"

Mom turned to the boys. With four brothers, I never got her attention for long.

I couldn't wait for my little sister to be born.

The last thing this world needed was another boy.

Chapter Eight

I pulled Honey's hand toward the den. "Come see my dad's pictures."

The den was cool and dark. I pointed at the pictures and certificates on the knotty pine walls. "He only takes pictures in black and white."

"Whoa." Honey breathed. "I see lots of colors. *Dolphin Grey*, and *Timberwolf Grey*, and *Moonbeam*!"

I hadn't noticed those greys before and wasn't sure what she meant, so I kept talking. "My dad teaches at the community college," I said proudly.

"What does he teach?" she asked.

"Biology. Ecology. And Typing."

"What's ecology?" She dragged her boots across the thick shag carpet and tipped her head back to see all the photos.

"It's about animals and their habitats."

"What's a habitat?" she asked.

"It's where you live," I said.

"A house?" Honey gawked at the pictures.

"I guess." The pictures were awful pretty. Even though Dad taught at the community college, he really wanted to be a photographer. He got a lot of his pictures in papers and magazines. And sometimes he wrote stories about them, too. There was one picture of my brother Jack holding a giant fish. One of the twins, Luke and Mark, in a canoe. A waterfall. A grey squirrel.

"A habitat is a house for us. But it's a creek for a fish. A tree for a squirrel."

The wall even had two pictures Jack had taken. Dad didn't trust the rest of us with his fancy camera.

Honey fidgeted with the handle on her lunchbox. "What about someone who doesn't have a home?"

"I don't know," I said. "I guess it's the place they are right then."

"What if that place doesn't feel like home?" she asked.

"Like when a fish is flopping in the grass?" I pictured Junior and me ice fishing this past winter, the slippery fish wriggling on top of the frozen lake, wildly trying to make their way back into the water. I was mad at Junior that day, wanting to throw the littlest fish back.

Then I thought about Junior with my snake at

Pitzel's. A hot and icky feeling started to simmer down at the pit of my belly.

"Kind of," Honey said, interrupting my thoughts. "But more like a tiger in a zoo."

I pictured the caged tiger at Fingal Family Animal Sanctuary and Amusement Park. Pacing back and forth, with only a few feet of space between him and the black bear next door. That tiger probably wanted to go back to Africa or India or wherever he came from.

I wondered what Honey's home was like. "I should probably walk you home. Won't your mom be worried about you?"

She shrugged and said, "I probably still have time for that snack."

In the kitchen, Honey ate her cookies slowly, carefully dunking each one in her glass, licking the milk dripping down her fingers. After she drained her glass and gulped the wet crumbs, she said I didn't need to walk her home.

I stood at the end of my driveway and watched her go. She drifted from one side of Limbo Creek Court to the other, making her way to the last house before the gravel dead-ended into the woods. The first five houses were lined up perfectly straight, like soldiers, standing close together. The Brooks house was a bit farther away at a slight angle. As if the other houses didn't want anything to do with it.

Honey gazed at the clouds and bent to study a rock or flower. But she never looked at her house. Or the weedy lawn. Or the saggy chain-link fence wrapped like a cage around the backyard.

I wasn't sure what kind of friend Honey would be, but I was sure of one thing—she had to be a better friend than Junior Greyhawk.

Chapter Nine

Saturday morning, I woke to the smell of coffee and bacon. And silence. The boys always slept in—I got Mom and Dad all to myself. I quickly shoved my pajamas and books under the bed and crammed my rock collection into a drawer.

I wanted room for the crib, just in case my parents decided to pull it out of the attic.

I spotted my Baby-Cries-A-Lot doll and yanked it out from under the bed. I put it on my dresser, spreading the dress around chubby, rubbery legs. Visions of my neat room—with just a few pink ruffles—and a smiling baby sister danced in my head as I rushed to the kitchen.

But on this particular Saturday, I didn't have Mom and Dad to myself. Matthew sat on Dad's lap. I slipped into a chair and glared at my youngest brother.

Mom set a plate in front of me.

Matthew smiled at me and announced, "I wet the bed!"

"Nice job," I mumbled, inching my plate away from him. I was ready to pinch my nose, but Dad's hand stroked Matthew's head and rested on top of a newspaper neatly folded next to his plate. The headline at the top of the newspaper said:

RARE CANADIAN LYNX SPOTTED?

I picked up the paper and read the article real careful. A wildcat was seen in Wampus Woods, north of Cameron Bridge. The hair on the back of my neck prickled. But it prickled even more when I saw the author.

I looked at Dad. "You wrote this article?"

Dad smiled and nodded. "I only wish there was a picture. Anders Erikson spotted some kind of wildcat while he was fishing. Someone else thought it was a mountain lion. But no one got a picture."

"A mountain lion?" Mom dropped her dish towel.

"I think it must have been a lynx," Dad said. "But I can't be sure."

I had to tell Honey about the lynx.

I shoved my plate away and pushed my chair back with a sudden screech. "I'm going to Honey's." Besides, I wanted to see what her mother and her house were like.

"Celie, wait," Mom said. Then she turned to Dad

and repeated, "A mountain lion?"

I stopped.

"A Canadian lynx," Dad said. "Or a bobcat. But there was something strange about its color. I think that it might have been an escaped pet."

Mom seemed to calm down then. "Celie, I need you to do something for me." She sat down on the kitchen chair with a *humph*. She picked up the dish towel and wiped her forehead. "I want you to take these cookies over to Mrs. Brooks to welcome Honey's family to the neighborhood."

I snatched the plate of cookies and rushed out the door.

I ran down the gravel driveway but froze halfway to the street.

There was someone near our mailbox.

In a striped tank top, shorts, socks pulled to his knees, and a new summer buzz-cut, stood Junior Greyhawk.

Chapter Ten

When I reached our mailbox, Junior put a hand on one hip and smirked like he knew a secret.

"What are *you* doing here?" I asked.

"What are *you* doing here?" he shot back.

"I live here—" I began.

Junior pulled out the newspaper that had been tucked under his arm. The same newspaper I read a few minutes before. He peered down the street, then turned back to me. "A Canadian lynx was spotted in Wampus Woods."

"Or a mountain lion," I said.

"It's huge. *Literally*. It's probably the biggest thing that's happened in this town. Ever." Junior rubbed his fingers across his stubby hair, reminding me of Rat Hurley. "You'll want to stay away from Wampus Woods with a wild animal roaming around."

"I'm not afraid!" But I thought of Cat-Scratch Clyde with his huge body and his huge wolf-dog and I shuddered.

Junior must have noticed my wobble because he said, "Maybe you should stick to dolls and tea parties."

"Junior Greyhawk!" I clenched my fists around the paper plate crushing a cookie under the plastic wrap. "You rotten, crazy, ugly, smelly picklehead!" And I only stopped there because I ran out of adjectives. Junior knew I wasn't the kind of girl who played with dolls—at least not anymore.

"*Chill out*," Junior said, sounding just like Rat.

"You don't get to tell me what to do!" I yelled, my face feeling hot. "For your information, this is going to be the best summer ever!"

"Oh yeah?" Junior scrunched his face. "What are you going to do? Play house and have picnics?"

I gripped the paper plate tight. We looked into each other's eyes and I was convinced he knew about my doll and the daydream of a pink ruffly bedroom to share with my new baby sister. My face grew hotter and I narrowed my eyes. I'd show Junior Greyhawk. "I'm going into Wampus Woods!" I shouted.

Junior shook his head. "You and what army?"

"Me and my best friend," I said looking past the big cottonwood, down the street toward Honey's little shack of a house. "Honey Brooks."

Junior looked shocked for a second but recovered

pretty quickly. "Me and Rat are going to do all sorts of exploring this summer. Stuff that's too dangerous for girls."

My head simmered and I clenched my teeth. I was no girly girl, but I wasn't sure if Honey liked to explore or climb trees. Maybe she even liked tea parties and dolls. But I couldn't let Junior get away with saying that. "Too dangerous?" I blurted. "I dare you to find the lynx first. We'll have teams. Me and Honey Brooks against you and Rat Hurley!"

I knew those weren't fair teams. Honey didn't know her way around the woods. Rat's mom was a taxidermist. Rat knew all about wild animals. I imagined moose and bear heads mounted on the walls of their double-wide trailer. Their glossy dead eyes looking down at Rat and his mother.

But I just couldn't let Junior win.

"You're too scared of the woods," Junior said, laughing between words. "I know you're scared of Cameron Bridge."

I glared at him. I should have never told him about Cameron Bridge. I had told him when we were friends.

I wasn't scared of the bridge exactly. It was the water.

I didn't know how to swim.

My brothers still teased me about swimming lessons at Loon Lake Community College when I wouldn't get in the pool. I sat on the edge with my arms crossed for eight Saturdays in a row. Junior knew about that.

"I'm not scared!" I lied.

"And what about Cat-Scratch Clyde?" Junior snickered. "Even Rat won't go anywhere near that crazy hermit."

"He doesn't scare me!" I lied again.

A great boat of a car pulled up, a big brown station wagon with fake wood paneling on the side. It was the car that had turned onto Cameron Bridge Road yesterday. "Leonard Junior," Junior's mom called from the car. "It's time to go."

I made a mental note of Junior's real name. *Leonard*. It might come in handy.

"It's a deal!" He hissed at me as his face flushed and his ears turned red.

Remembering what Dad said about wishing someone got a picture of the lynx, I stepped close and put my face right in Junior's. "Whoever gets a picture of the lynx first wins the dare!"

Part 2:
LIGHT & SHADOW

"Shine some light to get the shadows to disappear."

–McGill's Guide to Wildlife Photography

Chapter Eleven

Aunt Doreen said ten was old enough to pick out my own clothes without a serious fashion disaster and I didn't have to worry about pimples or boys. Obviously, she was wrong about the boys.

I rushed down Limbo Creek Court, trying not to fumble and drop the cookies onto the street. I had to convince Honey to come with me into Wampus Woods. There was no way I was going to get past Cat-Scratch Clyde alone. My brother Jack would never go. And my little brothers would wimp out. Even though she didn't look like it, Honey was tough.

She'd be my secret weapon.

I knocked on the front door. I had schemed all the way over about how to get Mrs. Brooks to invite me in for cookies. Hopefully, she wouldn't notice the two broken ones I slipped out from under the plastic wrap and into my pocket—we needed snacks for our trip into Wampus Woods.

When Mrs. Brooks came to the door, I felt like I was on the wrong side of a cowboy movie. She pointed a spray bottle like she was ready to shoot. Her face twisted up as if she just took a big old bite of raw rhubarb.

"Uhhhhh." I shuffled back a step.

"Well?" Mrs. Brooks stared at me. "We don't need no Girl Scout cookies. Run along." My heart skipped. Hadn't Honey mentioned me? I thought we were friends.

"These cookies are homemade," I started. Besides, who'd put Girl Scout cookies on a paper plate?

Then I remembered Aunt Doreen's advice about chit-chat and I kept going. "My mom wanted to welcome you to the neighborhood. She'd have come herself, but she's not feeling so hot. Her legs are swelling up like giant sausages. She's going to have a baby any day now. I want a girl. We have enough boys."

I paused for a minute. Her face was getting untwisted, so I started up again to see if I could get it to untwist all the way. "Anyway, if you ever need an egg or a cup of sugar, we've always got plenty. And you can come right to the front door. Mom says that's for grown-up guests. Kids have to go to the back." I suddenly clamped my mouth shut, thinking I should've gone to the back door. Maybe that's what got her face all sour.

I gave her my best smile, hoping my chipped tooth didn't show too much. "Can Honey come out and play?"

"She's busy." Mrs. Brooks took the cookies and swung the door. But I stuck my foot in quick.

"Can I wait?" I asked.

Mrs. Brooks sighed and must have taken another bite of that rhubarb because her face twisted up again. But she stepped back and pointed down a dark hall. Then she walked away.

I crept into the shadowy house. The smell of pine cleaner almost knocked me over. A cat meowed and pattered down the hall and I followed. It stopped and scratched a closed door.

The door squeaked open.

"Did *Mother* let you in?" Honey peeked toward the kitchen. I nodded. Honey grabbed my arm and pulled me in, quietly shutting the door.

"I followed the cat," I said.

"Nice Kitty." Honey was dressed in a stained tank top and ripped shorts and those red cowboy boots that were three sizes too big. She turned and smoothed the rumples from the bed. "I can't go out until my room is clean."

I looked around the sparse room. "It seems pretty clean to me. I usually just shove everything under the bed."

"Mother checks under the bed." Honey picked up the saddest doll ever. It was mostly bald and its cheeks were scribbled with green marker. The doll wore a diaper made from what looked like an old pair of flowered underwear. Honey hid the doll under her pillow and patted the pillow to smooth out the lumps.

"Done," she said. But then she picked at a piece of fuzz on her blanket and rubbed at a scuff on the floor. "Let's go outside. But be real quiet." Honey inched open the door and looked down the hall. She crept out of the bedroom and led the way toward the back of the house. We tip-toed down the dark hallway, trying not to make any noise.

Honey paused and peered around a corner into the kitchen.

"Come on," she whispered and pulled me the other way to the front door. But not before I saw Mrs. Brooks slide a bottle of beer behind the coffee pot.

Chapter Twelve

We left Honey's gloomy house and I blinked in the sunlight. It reminded me of going to the movies with Aunt Doreen on a Saturday afternoon. The way my eyes weren't used to the brightness and I'd squeeze them shut as Aunt Doreen held my hand and led me to her car. I didn't want to think about those Saturday afternoons, so I told Honey we were going into Wampus Woods.

"I thought you said that was off-limits." Honey followed me out to Limbo Creek Court like she had nowhere else to go, gazing up at the streaks of light streaming down through the leaves.

"The woods isn't off limits," I said. "Just Cameron Bridge and Blessed Sacrament Cemetery."

"But won't we have to cross Cameron Bridge?"

"Don't worry," I said, my stomach feeling a little

fluttery. "I'll figure something out."

"Why are we going into Wampus Woods?"

"Because Junior said exploring the woods is too dangerous for girls." I was still boiling with anger about that pudding-head Junior teaming up with Rat Hurley.

"So?" Honey shrugged.

I tried again, repeating Aunt Doreen's words. "Because ten is supposed to be the best age. I need an adventure."

Honey gazed at me with those bright blue eyes. "I've never been on an adventure."

But suddenly she wasn't looking at me anymore. She stared at the house next to hers. It was strange with all the front porch spindles painted different colors.

"*Mint Green*," Honey whispered. "And *Seafoam*."

"That's Arne Arneson's house," I said.

"What kind of name is that?" she asked.

"The kind who gives the best Halloween candy. He runs the paint machine at the hardware store."

"Whoa," said Honey. A Christmas wreath decorated with candy canes still hung from Mr. Arneson's front door.

"The next house is the Onstad's. They have a chocolate lab."

"Where they make chocolate?!" Honey's eyes grew wide.

"Not that kind of lab. The dog kind."

Honey's head drooped like a kid who lost her lucky quarter. So, I kept talking. "His name's Fluffy. It's a dumb name for a dog. Stay away from him when the fur on the back of his neck stands up. That means he's scared. He bites when he's scared." Honey looked worried, so I plowed ahead. "The next house is Freda Geagle's. She's the school secretary and a whole lot of other things. She doesn't have kids or pets. Just a raspberry patch. But watch out for the fireweed mixed in with the berries. It'll hurt."

Just then Freda Geagle walked out of her front door, carrying a baking dish wrapped in a kitchen towel. "My famous tater-tot hotdish!" She hummed as she shuffled toward Honey's house.

A blue car slowed and turned onto Limbo Creek Court.

"That's not anybody from around here," I said.

The car inched all the way down to the end and pulled into Honey's driveway.

A woman hauled a little girl out of the back and marched up to the front door. Right alongside Freda Geagle.

"My mother wants to start a daycare," Honey whispered. "That's why she's cleaning."

I thought about the beer behind the coffee pot.

It was as if Honey read my mind because she said, "She's not starting the daycare until next week."

Mrs. Brooks opened the front door all cheery. No more twisted rhubarb face.

"Wait," I said connecting the dots. "Is that what Mrs. Greyhawk was doing on our street this morning? The lady in the big brown car?"

Honey shrugged. "The doorbell rang, but Mother said to stay in my room."

Junior had a little sister. Maybe she was going to daycare. Junior seemed too old for daycare. And this would *not* be the best summer ever if Junior was hanging around Limbo Creek Court.

"Let's get ready for our adventure," I said.

We went to my house and made lists. Drew maps. Gathered bug spray, sun lotion, and a bottle of holy water. Holy water is supposed to keep bad things from happening. I'm not sure how it works, but I figured it was worth a try. I found it in Mom's top drawer, where it wasn't doing anybody any good under some frilly white hankies and a bunch of old Mother's Day cards.

My backpack was full and we were ready.

But my stomach hurt.

Not because I was scared or anything. I just wondered if the lynx was dangerous. Or if it really was a mountain lion looming behind the shady trees deep in Wampus Woods. I wondered about Cat-Scratch Clyde.

And I wondered if Junior was sharing secrets with Rat.

Chapter Thirteen

The rain pattered on and on, pinging against the window. Limbo Creek would be swelling. And there was no way I would be crossing Cameron Bridge after a big storm. Junior would be fishing anyway, not searching for the lynx.

It rained for three days straight. We had more time to plan, and my stomach felt better.

Honey and I sprawled across the shag carpet in the den. Dad sat at his desk grading papers. I was busy thinking about the best way to ask him if I could borrow his camera.

Dad was proud of his camera. He polished it with a special cloth and stored it in a fancy leather case with extra lenses.

Honey and I re-read the newspaper article to get ready for our trip into Wampus Woods. Actually, I read and Honey drew in a ratty old notebook she kept in her Snoopy lunchbox. That lunchbox was crammed with all kinds of colors: *Cornflower Blue*, *Jade Green*, and her favorite, *Lemon Yellow*. She copied some of the photos lining the wall.

Each picture pulled you in with its own story. Even the picture of the old picnic table outside Pitzel's Loaf & Bait. It was my least favorite picture. You could tell it was early evening because of the sun and the shadows. And you could tell that somebody had just eaten ice cream, with the yucky melted streaks across the worn planks. Bottles were piled in the grass, which meant that Midge Pitzel set them so Cat-Scratch Clyde wouldn't have to dig through the dumpster for them.

I studied the photos Jack had taken. If I got a picture of the Canadian lynx, maybe Dad would hang it up in his den. In other families, turning twelve meant you got to sit in the front seat of the car. Or babysit. In our family, it meant you got to use Dad's camera.

Twelve seemed a long way off.

I showed Honey the ragged old *Illustrated Encyclopedia of the Modern World*, book 10, L to M. "Lynx, a wildcat with short tail and long tapering ears belonging to the family *Felide* and genus *Lynx*." I wasn't sure how to pronounce Felide, but I figured Honey didn't know the difference.

Unfortunately, Dad did. "It's pronounced FEEEE–Lide."

Honey turned to me. "Is it dangerous?" she asked.

"It doesn't say." I skimmed through the next paragraph. "Listen to this. The Canadian lynx, *L. canadensis*, is a larger, much more robust and shaggy wildcat, resembling the lynx of Siberia."

"Can–uh–DENS–us," said Dad absently as he flipped through more papers.

"Whoa," said Honey, staring at her notebook. She sketched a scary version of Nice Kitty, with *Timberwolf Grey* tufts on the ears sticking out against a *Robin Egg Blue* sky.

"Yeah. Large. Robust. Shaggy. Sounds dangerous." I snapped the encyclopedia shut. Honey flinched.

"Is there just one lynx in Wampus Woods?" Honey asked.

"I think so," I said.

"Where there's one, there's probably more," Dad said.

Honey and I stared at each other wide-eyed.

I hadn't thought of that.

"So, there could be a whole pack of them?" I wasn't so sure about going into Wampus Woods with even *one* shaggy and robust wildcat.

"Maybe." Dad rested his elbows on his knees, leaning toward us. "Do you know what you call a group of wildcats?"

I shook my head.

"There are two different words. A dowt . . ." He

paused. "Or a destruction!"

Honey's eyes bulged wider.

"Which word should we use?" I asked.

"It doesn't matter," he said.

"Why not?"

"Because I *DOWT* they would know the difference!" He laughed and turned back to his desk.

I rolled my eyes at Honey and giggled. It was fun having her for a friend. And Mom and Dad had stopped looking all sad and worried about me being the only girl in the fourth grade.

I browsed through the books on Dad's shelf, trying to look real casual. I wondered if he would let me use the camera if I asked real nice.

"This book looks charming," I said, trying out a nice word. "What's it about?"

Dad raised one eyebrow. "*McGill's Guide to Wildlife Photography*? It's a guide to wildlife photography."

I rolled my eyes so that Honey could see but Dad couldn't. "Are there lynx in this book?"

"Maybe." Dad picked up a stack of papers. "Use the index."

A typical Dad-answer. I blew out a big breath. But I opened to the index in *McGill's Guide to Wildlife Photography* and skimmed the pages.

"Landscape. Lenses. Light. Lions. Luminance. Lynx!" I shouted and flipped quickly to page 115. I scanned the text, noticing how someone had penciled notes in the margins.

"Celie, did you have another question for me?" Dad took off his glasses and dragged his hand through his messy hair. "I have to get some things done for the class I'm teaching this summer."

"What class?" I asked. Dad usually got the whole summer off. Why else would anyone want to be a teacher?

He flipped through his camera manual. "The photography class."

My heart thunked and I closed *McGill's Guide* with a snap. This was my chance to ask for the camera, but I had just been hit with a truckload of bricks.

Dad was teaching Junior's photography class.

Chapter Fourteen

I clutched *McGill's Guide to Wildlife Photography* and blurted the first thing that came into my head, "Can I borrow this book?" Then without waiting for Dad to answer, I ran to my room.

Honey hurried after me and asked, "What's luminance?"

My mind was on Dad teaching the photography class, so I was confused by her question.

"From the index," Honey prompted.

So, we sat on my bed and hunched over the book. There were six basic lessons to wildlife photography. The first was about choosing your subject. I already knew that my subject was the lynx. Besides, that chapter was probably for complete beginners. So, I skipped to the second lesson: Light & Shadow.

I read from page 22: "*Photographs cannot replicate*

the range of brightness, called luminance, of most subjects in the wild."

"Like light and dark colors!" Honey said, all excited.

But I didn't care about the colors. "Let's look up lynx!" I quickly shuffled to page 115. Covering half the page was a photograph of a Canadian lynx resting next to a half-eaten, bloody pile of fur.

"Do you think that lynx killed that animal?" Honey whispered, pointing to the picture.

I read the text. *"The Alaska wilderness is a refuge for Canadian lynx, although visitors to this wilderness are unlikely to see one due to their elusive nature."*

"What does that mean?" asked Honey.

"Number one, our lynx is a long way from home," I said. "And number two, it'll be hard to find."

Honey added, "And number three, it might be real hungry."

I read the pencil marks in the margins, hand-written lightly in cursive. "Last blue lynx spotted 100 years ago. Lynx = secrets in Native legends."

"A blue lynx?" Honey asked.

But I didn't answer, because this loopy cursive wasn't Dad's handwriting. It was swirly and fancy. Dad always wrote in neat block letters. I dug in my pocket for the crumpled note, wrapped around my ten-dollar bill. I had kept them both safe in my pocket since my last birthday.

The swirly and fancy handwriting on the baby blue stationery read: "How you spend a crispy ten-dollar bill says a lot about a person." It was the same as the handwriting in the book.

Shaking a little, I slid the note and ten-dollar bill between the pages of *McGill's Guide to Wildlife Photography*. Then I closed the book and slipped it into my backpack. I grabbed some change hidden in my sock drawer and shoved it in my pocket.

We needed more supplies—mosquito nets and candy from Pitzel's Loaf & Bait.

I pulled Honey to the back door. She clutched her Snoopy lunchbox as we hustled down the driveway, still damp from three days of rain.

Camera or no camera, I had to find out about the blue lynx and I knew exactly who to ask—Gerty Bigheart.

Part 3: PERSPECTIVE

"Know where to stand. You never really see your subject until you consider all possible points of view."

—McGill's Guide to Wildlife Photography

Chapter Fifteen

We marched down Limbo Creek Court and onto County Road 2 and I told Honey a little about my Aunt Doreen. About how she always wore a feather in her hat, hated turtle necks, and loved butter-brickle ice cream.

Honey was a real good listener. Until a *Burnt Orange* butterfly fluttered by. She wandered off, clomping after the butterfly in her *Brick Red* cowboy boots.

And then I told Honey about how a camera works. About how we needed film to put into the camera.

Honey tipped her head back so the sun shone against her face. She took a deep breath, closed her eyes, and smiled. I was beginning to think she wasn't listening, but she suddenly asked, "What's film?"

I knew all about film from Dad. So, I explained.

"It's this dark plastic tape stuff that fits into the camera. When you snap a picture, the image is burned onto the film."

While Honey caught fluff drifting down from the cottonwood trees, I continued. "Once we have a whole roll of pictures taken, we'll take the film to Chet's Drugstore in town and wait three weeks for them to develop it into paper pictures. It'll be part of the adventure."

"I've never had a real adventure," Honey said, holding her arms out straight and twirling down the road.

"According to my Aunt Doreen, even a walk through the woods can turn into an adventure with the right attitude."

"Until I moved here," Honey began, "I'd never even been in the woods."

"Never *ever*?" I asked.

"Not even once." She shook her head. "We lived in a basement apartment. Mother called it garden-level, but there were no gardens. No trees. Just a parking lot."

I was quiet for a minute, thinking about how *McGill's Guide to Wildlife Photography* said you had to get away from the parking lots and into nature for the best view. Then my mind wandered to the handwriting in the book and how it could be the same as the loopy writing on the note with my ten-dollar bill.

"I would love a garden," Honey said.

Luckily, by then we had reached Pitzel's Loaf & Bait so I didn't have to talk about gardens or think about the weird fluttery feeling in my stomach. I would find out about the blue lynx.

"Hi, Gerty," I said as soon as I pushed through the door. "We need supplies. And advice."

"It's a popular day for supplies," Gerty said. But I was more interested in her advice, not her supplies. Only not all Gerty's advice was good, like the summer she told Midge to stock spicy ketchup. People around here liked their food bland. They thought French fries were exotic. Spicy ketchup was a real stretch. Some of those bottles were still on the shelf covered in dust.

"Where would you go to look for a blue lynx?" I asked slowly, watching her face for a reaction.

"Blue lynx?" Her head shot up so fast, her glasses slipped off her nose. "Who told you about that?"

"It's just something I heard," I said carefully, still watching her reaction.

"Well, you can just stop wondering." She started cleaning the counter like she was angry at the rag.

"Why?" I pressed her.

"Because a blue lynx only happens once every hundred years." She paused and looked out the window.

"But maybe—" I began.

"There's no maybe," she shot back.

"Why is it blue?" Honey whispered in Gerty's direction, hiding behind me.

Gerty looked at her for a second before saying, "It isn't really. A blue lynx is an albino. It has no pigment, no color."

"White?" Honey asked.

"Kind of," Gerty said.

"Like a black and white photo?" I asked, thinking about *McGill's Guide to Wildlife Photography*.

"Not with the lynx," Gerty said. "An albino lynx is whitish or greyish with just a hint of blue. My grandfather told me he saw a blue lynx pelt once. But that was years ago. That's when I heard the legend."

"What legend?" Honey and I asked together.

But before we could hear more, another customer walked in. We walked over to the pickles and hotdog buns. The bait tanks in the back of the store bubbled loudly. Midge rolled a toothpick around in her mouth while she scooped up some minnows. As we waited for the customer to leave, we turned down the next aisle, breathing in the mix of chocolate and fishy bait. Honey followed behind me gawking as if we were in a giant toy shop.

"Can we get chocolate?" Honey asked. I swear she was almost drooling like Fluffy or Darwin.

"Chocolate will melt," I said.

Her shoulders drooped. And I wondered what it was like, living in a dingy house, with a mean mother, and a crummy doll with green marker smeared all over its face.

I grabbed a small paper bag from the candy stand. "We'll get two pieces of chocolate and eat them before it gets too hot." I had enough change for candy and could save the ten-dollar bill.

We picked out two chocolates, two Pixy Stix, and two Slo-Pokes. A snort came from behind the stacks of Bottle Caps and Milk Duds, sounding kind of like a pig rooting around in the mud. Or someone trying hard to hold in a laugh. Honey and I walked around the other side of the candy stand.

With a smirky face and mouthful of toffee stood Junior Greyhawk.

Chapter Sixteen

Junior stuffed another toffee into his mouth and smiled.

"You didn't pay for that!" I said, wondering what part of our conversation with Gerty he overheard.

"Free sample," he whispered between chews. He sounded just like Rat Hurley.

"Then why are you whispering?!" I said loudly.

"Hey, be quiet! I don't want Midge the Fridge coming after me." He glanced toward the back of the store. "Check this out." Junior held up a brand-new camera with a shiny lens and thick blue-green strap.

"*Aquamarine*," Honey whispered.

The strap was beaded like a wampum belt, in a pattern that probably told some kind of story.

"Where did you get that?" I asked.

"My parents," Junior said.

"Is it your birthday?" Honey gawked at the camera.

"Nah," he said. "They'll buy me anything. *Literally.* I told them I needed it for the photography class. You should've signed up, Celie. You had your chance."

"Oh yeah?" I said. "I don't need a class. My dad can teach me everything." Except Dad didn't have much time for me lately. It was a good thing I had *McGill's Guide*.

"I heard you were looking for advice," Junior said all superior. He tossed a candy wrapper onto the floor and grabbed a Tootsie Pop. "So, here's some advice. Stick with black and white film. Color film is too expensive for amateurs."

"I'm not an amateur!" I thought he was about to unwrap the Tootsie Pop, but he slowly moved it toward his pocket. He glanced over at Midge.

"You already had your free sample, *Leonard* Junior." I grabbed for the Tootsie Pop, but my hand swiped too low.

"Hey! Watch it!" He jumped back, knocking over a tower display of sun lotion.

It got a bit crazy after that. Midge yelled and shook her fist at Junior. Her minnow net flew out of her hand, spraying stinky fish-bait water. Then she slipped.

Gerty rushed over from behind the counter and nearly did the splits on the slippery floor. And Gerty was no gymnast.

Junior sprinted out the door.

Through the window, I saw Junior swing his leg back to kick the pop machine. He looked up at Rat Hurley standing with his arms crossed in the middle of County Road 2. Junior stopped mid-kick. I got an icky sickly feeling in the pit of my belly when I saw Junior swagger out to meet Rat.

So, I busied myself helping Gerty and Midge pick up the mess.

Midge rubbed her hip through her husky jeans. "This place is going to smell fishy for months," she grumbled.

"But this place always smells fishy," I said. Midge looked at me with an Oscar-the-Grouch face so I kept talking. "Anyway, I was wondering about the lynx."

"Beef links?" Gerty asked. "They're in aisle three. Next to the prune juice." And when Gerty started talking about the benefits of prune juice, I remembered Aunt Doreen's advice about awkward conversations and changed the subject. Real quick.

"Not beef links. Canadian lynx," I said. "I want to hear about the legend."

Gerty sighed. "The blue lynx is a sign. A symbol. The Creator is sending someone a message." She gazed up at the ceiling and talked in a soft and mysterious voice. "Lynx are supposed to know our secrets...." Her voice trailed off as she closed her eyes, trying to connect with something other-worldly.

But a fly landed on Gerty's nose and her eyes snapped open. She swatted at it and said, "We got some new bug spray this season, but I hear it works better on mosquitos than flies." She chatted on about bug spray and which brand of aspirin sold best.

She wouldn't talk about the lynx anymore and we were left wondering what kind of secrets she meant.

Chapter Seventeen

Looking at the water gushing under Cameron Bridge made my stomach fluttery. Aunt Doreen's warning about how it was dangerous still whispered in my ears and I wondered now if she wasn't talking about either the bridge or the boys, but about Cat-Scratch Clyde.

We turned down the overgrown lane next to the bridge. It led to Clyde's place, so we only walked a few yards.

The shade and the breeze felt cool against my skin.

Honey leaned down to smell the pinkish-white petals of a flower.

"Look," she said. "It's *Wild Strawberry.*"

I crouched down near her. I wanted to see the flower from her angle because *McGill's Guide* said that sometimes it's good to change perspective—or look at something from a different place. "It's a Lady's-slipper," I corrected.

"I mean the color," she said. "Why is it called a Lady's-slipper?"

"I suppose it's because it kind of looks like something you'd put on a foot," I answered.

"Like a ballet shoe!" Honey studied the tiny petals.

"I guess," I said. "Gerty calls them moccasin flowers."

She stood up after a while and we walked deeper into the shade. With the tree cover, it was cooler here, only dappled sun sparkling through the leaves. The birds chirped and squawked.

The further we got, the faster my heart beat.

Soon we stepped into a misty and magical clearing. Neat rows of apple trees lined the far side. Vegetables popped out of the ground in curvy rows. Stones were piled in different patterns. Trails, just wide enough for one person, twisted through the flowers and trees.

"Whoa," Honey breathed.

We listened. Chirping. Buzzing. Wind gently rattling the trees.

Honey pointed to white wooden beehives nestled between the apple trees. We moved slowly toward the bees, drawn to the musical whir of their wings.

But then Honey tugged at my sleeve and pointed to a sign:

NO TRESPASSING!

Just beyond the sign was Clyde's home. A shack, actually. The paint was blistered like it had been out in the sun too long. A few black shingles hung crookedly. One window was boarded up.

"We should go back," I whispered. I didn't want Darwin the dog—or Cat-Scratch Clyde—chasing us.

Suddenly Clyde stepped out from behind a shed, wearing a pointed hat with mosquito netting covering his face.

I almost wet my pants.

We stood still. So did Clyde, staring at us for a full minute.

And then we did the only thing that made sense.

We ran.

Chapter Eighteen

We had a routine over the next week. Honey would show up at my back steps. I didn't go to her house since her mother seemed real sour about everything. Then we'd walk to Pitzel's Loaf & Bait. We'd get some supplies or advice from Gerty and Midge. Then we'd hike as deep into the woods as we dared. But we didn't go near Clyde . . . or Junior and Rat.

Honey brought her Snoopy lunchbox everywhere. I figured it would be up to me if we were going to survive in the woods, so I filled my backpack with all kinds of things. Flashlight. Bug spray. Rope. Band-aids. Matches. Baloney sandwiches.

After about two weeks of this routine, we were running low on snacks and covered in mosquito bites. Things weren't going so good.

Honey took off her cowboy boots and hopped for a while, trying to miss the sharp rocks in the road. We searched for tracks, hoping they would lead us to the lynx.

"Don't you have sneakers?"

"My daddy's gonna buy me some when he gets home."

I doubted that. So, the next day I gave Honey a pair of my old tennis shoes. I also gave her the shiny black tap shoes I had outgrown. She preferred the tap shoes.

We weren't having much luck finding the lynx, but one thing was sure—we were a step ahead of Rat and Junior. Instead of getting clues about the lynx, they ate candy from Pitzel's Loaf & Bait and threw rocks off Cameron Bridge.

On another day, sticky with sweat, Honey and I slogged through a stretch of Cameron Bridge Road lined with wild sumac. Honey zig-zagged from one thing to the next, as if she was looking for a bug instead of a lynx. She studied every weed. Sometimes she just stopped, closed her eyes, and breathed in the air.

I linked arms with her and marched down the middle of the road. We giggled when Honey started a chorus line kick. I followed along.

"When my daddy comes home, he's gonna sign me up for dance lessons," said Honey. "Then I'll be a ballerina!"

"But those are tap shoes," I said. "Anyway, when's your dad coming home?"

"Soon." She kicked higher. "But Mother doesn't want me talking about that."

I stopped high-kicking. "Why not?"

She stood still and looked to the tops of the trees as if she were thinking of a real good answer. She rubbed her knee, where she had banged it against the gravel. She had a long bruise, wrapped snake-like around the back of her leg.

She saw me looking, then rushed over to a big log and sat, her calves tucked tight against the log.

I joined her and we swung our legs. My sneakers, then her tap shoes. Back and forth, back and forth.

The yellow sun blazed above us.

"Is that luminance?" Honey asked, peering up at the sky.

"I suppose," I said, shielding my eyes from the brightness.

"Do you think we'll find the lynx?" she asked.

"If it doesn't go extinct before the end of the summer," I said, bummed that our adventure was such a dud.

"But the encyclopedia didn't say that." Honey looked startled.

"Yeah," I said. "But that encyclopedia is a million years old."

The chirping of the birds slowed.

Flies buzzed.

"I hope we never find the lynx," Honey finally whispered.

I couldn't believe she said that. We'd been looking for two solid weeks. It was our goal. "Why?" I asked.

Honey swung her feet.

She clutched that Snoopy lunchbox.

I thought about her sad house and nasty mother. I thought about her bruised and sore legs, turning slightly yellow on the edge. I remembered the bruise on her forehead when Darwin chased us into the woods.

Then a thought hit me so hard I had to grab hold of the log.

Those bruises had already started to yellow. Those bruises were old.

And they weren't from falling or rubbing against her boots.

She looked down and whispered so quietly that I barely heard. "Because this has already been my best summer ever." She tipped her head back and looked straight into the sun. "A *Lemon Yellow* summer."

Chapter Nineteen

Honey and I leaned back and let the sun warm our faces. Tears pricked the corners of my eyes as I thought about Honey having to live in that gloomy house. I closed my eyes. I sure wished Aunt Doreen was here to give me advice.

As the bright sun shone reddish-orange against my eyelids, I daydreamed about Aunt Doreen. If she were around, she'd take Honey and me out for ice cream. We'd tell her everything. She'd have all the right answers. Maybe she'd even help us find the lynx.

But she wasn't here. I was on my own.

"Well, well, well," said a deep voice. "Look what we have here."

I came out of my daydreaming and squinted at the road.

Rat Hurley swaggered toward us in cowboy boots

like he was ready for a shoot-out. And maybe he was. Because over his left shoulder was a BB gun.

Junior walked behind him, pushing that pink bike.

They came to a stop in front of us. Close. A little too close.

Rat glared at us over his aviator sunglasses. "Look, Junior." He nodded his head toward me and Honey. "Some girls. Maybe you want to join them for a tea party."

Junior scowled and his upper lip curled back like he smelled something stinky.

I glanced back and forth between Junior and Rat Hurley . . . and that gun.

"What do you say, Le-NERD?" Rat said. "It's time to find that lynx. Gonna come with me or play with the girls?"

No one said anything, but Junior's ears turned bright red. I wondered how Rat found out Junior's real name.

"I'm peelin' outta here." Rat gazed into the woods and said, "I figure my mom will look classy in a lynx coat, so I'm going to Pitzel's to grab some of Nerdy Gerty's hotdogs. For lynx bait. Coming, Le-NERD?"

Then he swaggered away without waiting for Junior to answer.

Junior picked up his pink bicycle, looked at us with a sad face, and scurried after Rat.

I wondered why Junior stayed friends with that

creep. I mean, Junior might have been creepy lately, but Rat was a first-rate, full-grown Creep with a capital C.

"What are they going to do with that gun?" Honey hopped off the log.

"I don't know. But we'd better beat them to the lynx."

I needed to think, but the little bit of advice from Gerty and a section on stalking wildlife in *McGill's Guide* were all muddled with thoughts of that BB gun.

Could a BB gun kill a lynx?

Chapter Twenty

We waited until Junior and Rat were out of sight and started toward home, stopping at the parking lot outside Pitzel's Loaf & Bait. Midge peered out the dirty windows with a scowl on her face. Sticky ketchup packets littered the parking lot.

The ketchup made me think about the hotdogs that spun around and around in the roller next to Gerty's front counter. The hotdogs that rolled all day long and got nowhere. But they still turned and turned and turned. I felt a bit like a hotdog. We were doing a lot of moving, but getting nowhere.

We walked into the store, just as Rat and Junior walked out. They each had a hotdog and bulging pockets. Probably ketchup packets.

"Rat thinks he's so cool with those sunglasses," I muttered as we walked by the counter.

"Cool doesn't last," Gerty said. "Before you know it,

diet pop sounds cool. Then yoga. Next, you're excited about reading glasses and prune juice."

I cringed when she mentioned prune juice again.

"Junior's camera is cool," said Honey. "I bet it takes real colorful pictures."

"We don't even have a camera." I sighed. Dad's camera was tucked safely in his fancy case in the den and would probably stay that way. "Boys get all the breaks."

"I'm sure you'll figure it out," Gerty said. But I stopped next to the bait buckets with my head down. Gerty continued, "You can sit in the mud, but you don't need to water the weeds."

"What?" I asked, wondering what she was getting at.

"Go ahead and feel your feelings," Gerty said. "But don't wallow in them." She pointed to the back of the store. Midge's head was following a fish across the tank like she was a cat. "Do you think Midge just mopes around hoping to sell bait? No. She doubles the price on nightcrawlers when she knows the sunfish are biting."

Honey gazed into the plexiglass container with the day-old donuts.

Gerty shifted her reading glasses down her nose. "Do you see Midge's bowling shirt?"

I nodded.

"Do you think that me and Midge mope when we

get a gutter ball? No. We double down and win the bowling league."

"But you've won like fifteen years in a row," I said.

"Eighteen." Gerty glared at me over her glasses. "That's not the point. The point is, it's time to climb out of the mud."

"Gerty?" Honey said shyly.

"Yes, sweetie?" Gerty leaned forward on the counter, giving Honey all her attention.

"What do you do with the day-old donuts the day after they're day-old?"

Gerty reached over and picked up a paper bag, folded over neatly at the top. "Sometimes I give them to Clyde, but today I saved these just for you."

Honey's extra big smile at Gerty's gift of two-day-old donuts made me feel all warm and fuzzy inside. But before I could feel too many feels, I got caught up at the mention of Clyde. I just knew we needed to go deeper into the woods to find the lynx.

"Is Cat-Scratch Clyde crazy?" I blurted, wanting to know if he was as dotty as people said, because his shack stood between us and the rest of Wampus Woods.

After those words were out of my mouth, I remembered Aunt Doreen's advice. She said to pause and count to five before you say anything that might hurt someone's feelings.

But I wasn't good at pausing.

Chapter Twenty One

Gerty stopped wiping donut crumbs off the counter. "His name is Clyde Nygard." She bent her head under the counter so I could no longer see her.

I got worried she might be getting an ax or something, or that her feelings were hurt when I called Clyde crazy. "I didn't mean it that way. I just . . . Junior and Rat said he was crazy and walks around without shoes all winter long . . . and that he raises wolves. And that he's meaner than a jackrabbit. . . except jackrabbits aren't really that mean . . . and did you know that a jackrabbit can jump ten feet? And I just . . . wanted to know what Clyde was like."

"Let me give you some advice," she said popping up from behind the counter. "Don't believe everything those boys tell you." She bent and scrounged under the counter some more. Then she stuck her foot up next to the cash register. "Do you see my purple socks?"

"Yes."

"And you know I always wear purple socks, right?"

"Yes."

"Am I crazy?"

Gerty looked a bit crazy. But I wasn't about to say so. "No," I said.

"So, if I wear purple socks every day, and I'm not crazy, why would Clyde be crazy because he goes barefoot every day?"

I didn't really follow her logic. I was about to say that at least she wore shoes over her purple socks. But I stopped myself. "I don't know," I mumbled.

"Besides," she said. "He wears boots in January."

"I'm sorry." I looked down. Honey stood next to me. I stared at her *Brick Red* boots.

"Some people are just different," Gerty said. "And you have to make up your *own* mind about them. Clyde's timid around people. He's better with animals. Here. Take this."

She handed me a faded old brochure. I wiped off the dust. It read:

WILDCAT WONDERLAND

Box 28 Cameron Bridge Road

Family friendly entertainment.

Wildcats in action.

Tigers. Lions. Bobcat. Lynx.

I read that last line twice.

Tigers. Lions. Bobcat. Lynx.

"Wildcat Wonderland was a long time ago," Gerty said. "Before you were born."

"Does he still have wildcats?" I'd heard so many rumors about Cat-Scratch Clyde and his wild beasts.

Gerty shook her head sadly. "Clyde ran Wildcat Wonderland with his brothers. Norbert and Ned. We lost them both in the war. The big one. There was no Wildcat Wonderland after that."

My skin prickled thinking about Clyde and his dead brothers, their spirits roaming the woods. And then my skin prickled even more imagining Wildcat Wonderland. "What happened to the wildcats?"

Gerty shook her head and gazed out the window. As if she was looking at something far away.

Honey and I waited, listening to the tick-tick-tick of the Hamm's Beer clock and the gurgle of the bait tanks.

Gerty's voice broke into my thoughts. "Only Clyde knows. Maybe the wildcats are still out there."

Chapter Twenty Two

Outside of Pitzel's Loaf & Bait, Honey and I hopped around the ketchup splatters all the way across the parking lot.

Honey peeked into the paper bag. "Whoa! Cinnamon sugar!" She pulled a donut out of the bag and offered it to me.

I shook my head. "Those are two-day-old donuts."

"They're still good." She took a big bite, then licked the sugar crystals off her lips. I unfolded the Wildcat Wonderland brochure.

"If Clyde had wildcats, he would know if it was a mountain lion or a lynx." I scanned the woods. "He would know what they ate. Where they slept. I wonder if they sleep in trees?"

"It would be nice to sleep in a tree." Honey tipped her head back to face the treetops.

"It would be cold and mosquitoey." I slapped at a fly with the brochure. "It's much nicer to sleep in your own bed. And a tree would be creepy at night. Things sneaking up on you. Scary sounds."

"Oh." Honey looked away. "I thought it would be different sleeping outside."

I wasn't sure what she meant. Maybe her house was full of scary sounds. "You'd fall out of a tree." I pointed out, still feeling a little uneasy about what went on in her house.

Honey was quiet, so as we hiked north on Cameron Bridge Road, I chit-chatted about scary ghost stories. "My brother Jack says that Blessed Sacrament Cemetery is haunted. By the ghost of Lucky Lindstrom who stayed out fishing all night during a full moon. When he finally came home, the table was set with pork chops and corn on the cob. His wife sat at the other end of the table—dead." I paused as we looked through the cemetery gates. "Now the ghost of Lucky Lindstrom comes to visit his wife's grave whenever there's a full moon."

Honey found a caterpillar on the road and watched it for a while. Then she cradled it and moved it to a leaf where it wouldn't get squashed.

"I love ghost stories," I said, even if they made me shudder. "But Junior hates them. I can't figure him out. One day he's fine and the next day he's kicking that pop machine. Probably too much sugar."

There was so much I didn't seem to get lately. About Junior. About Clyde. About Honey.

Honey picked up a lone turkey feather, the only hint a turkey had ever been there.

"Did you know the Sioux used turkey feathers for arrows? Aunt Doreen told me that. She also told me that they used lamb's ear for diapers." I thought about the texture of the lamb's ear leaves and how that texture might look on film.

"Lamb's ears?" Honey asked. "How'd they do that?"

"Not real lamb's ears. It's a plant, with leaves that are all soft and fuzzy. Perfect for a baby." Like our new baby.

I hadn't thought about having a little sister for a while. I hadn't thought about Mom much either. Or Aunt Doreen. Lately, all my thoughts were wrapped up in the search for the lynx. A little pang of loneliness hit me just then as I thought of Mom and Aunt Doreen and how we used to do so much together.

"What color are they?" Honey asked.

"What color are what?"

"The lamb's ears. What color are they?" Honey closed her eyes as she walked, as if trying to picture the leaves.

"Green," I said.

"What kind of green?" she asked.

"I don't know." My feelings were making me uncomfortable and I was eager to get back to our search.

But I stopped, took a deep breath, and closed my eyes. I pictured the fuzzy green and silvery leaves as I'd seen them that day last October when Aunt Doreen told me the story about the Sioux and their babies and the lamb's ear diapers. The misty breeze brushed against my bare arms on that otherwise warm day. Aunt Doreen's hand gently squeezed my shoulder.

"*October Mist,*" I whispered to Honey.

"*October Mist* sounds like the perfect color!" Honey said. "Do you think Clyde has some lamb's ear in his garden?"

Honey's excitement made me realize something. I had been trying to find this lynx all alone, thinking Honey was just tagging along for the ride, trying to steer clear of her nasty mother.

But we were a team.

I needed real live people to win this dare.

I felt the lingering touch of Aunt Doreen's hand on my shoulder, and Gerty's words echoing in my ears.

I grabbed Honey's hand and said, "Let's go find out!"

Part 4: COMPOSITION & BACKGROUND

"There is something magic about the number three. Art, literature, and photography come to life with the rule of thirds."

–McGill's Guide to Wildlife Photography

Chapter Twenty Three

Honey danced and swirled all the way to Cameron Bridge, stopping only once to carefully step over an ant hill.

"Maybe Clyde still has some wildcats in cages," I said.

We turned down the cool and dark path that led to Clyde's place. An old wood sign leaned against a tree. I paused to brush the vines away. *Wildcat Wonderland.* I hadn't noticed the sign with faded letters the last time we went down this trail.

Honey suddenly hurried ahead of me. It was hard to keep her away from all those colors. I tried to catch up, but by the time I got to the clearing, Honey was weaving in and out of the garden trails looking at hollyhocks and ferns and lamb's ear. Honey squatted and cradled a coneflower blossom gently in her palms and leaned in to breathe in its scent.

Even though I wanted to follow her, I glanced around nervously, worried that Clyde wouldn't exactly be happy to see us.

"I wondered when you'd come back," said a voice from behind us.

Honey and I jumped.

Clyde was leaning against a run-down shed. He shuffled his bare feet over to the screen door, squeaked it open, and reached inside.

I almost bolted, imagining him reaching for a rifle. But he pulled off his hat and stuck it inside the shed and strode toward us with those long, pole legs.

My heart beat fast, but I didn't move.

"So, you want to know more about wildcats." His green eyes sparkled when he said wildcats.

"Yes," I squeaked, wondering how he knew.

He zigzagged through a trail to the shack and we followed. He sat on a bench. "You girls want something to drink?"

I *was* thirsty but shook my head, wary of anything he was offering.

"Suit yourself." He shrugged and reached into an old metal cooler, grabbed a brown bottle, and took a long swig.

"Is that beer?" Honey asked, hiding behind me.

"Root beer," he said. "I make it myself."

I watched the water droplets drip down the side of

the bottle.

Honey gently smacked her lips. "Where do you get the bottles?" she asked.

"They're recycled," he said. And I was glad I had turned him down. Everyone knew he sifted through the dumpsters at Pitzel's Loaf & Bait.

Honey leaned in closer to me and said, "I know where you can get lots of brown bottles."

I thought about the bottle behind the coffee pot at Honey's house. Clyde raised one eyebrow.

I changed the subject, hoping to sound smart. "We'd like to know the habits of the FEEEE-Line CanaDENsis." But even if I did pronounce it right, I got my words mixed up.

Clyde paused, the bottle halfway to his lips. He looked over at me.

"The *Lynx canadensis* of the family *Felide* doesn't usually make it south of the Canadian border around here," he said.

"Why is it here?" Honey asked.

"Yeah," I said, thinking about how the newspaper article said the lynx, or some kind of wildcat, was spotted in Wampus Woods. "Canada is a hundred miles away."

His eyes twinkled. "The Canadian lynx doesn't have to go through border control."

"Where does it sleep?" I studied the woods around me. "In trees?"

"No," he said and took another long drink.

I figured I would have to work harder to get information from him, like how you have to work real hard to squeeze the last bit of toothpaste out of the tube.

"On the ground?" I asked

"Yes," he said.

"Do they dig dens?" I asked.

"No," he said. "They'll use a natural dip in the ground surrounded by bushes. A downed tree. A pile of logs."

I made a mental note of all the places a lynx might be hiding.

"What does it eat? Can it climb trees? Is there more than one?" The questions shot out of me like air squealing out of a balloon.

"They like snowshoe hare best," he said.

"What do they like second best?" I asked, hoping it wasn't people.

"Small vermin." He scratched his ear.

He talked on a bit. His words soothed gently as he spoke of the lynx and the woods. A cool breeze tickled my face as I gazed across the magical garden. It felt like a fairy tale.

"Lynx are like people in some ways." Clyde finished his root beer and stood. "They need the same things that we do. Food. Water. Shelter. A little companionship once in a while."

I felt sorry for Clyde then. I wondered if he missed the brothers he lost in the war. A cloud floated over, putting half the garden in shade and I sensed a heavy mood as the three of us sat silently for a long time.

"If you want to find the lynx," Clyde said, "look for those things."

Then, without saying goodbye, he shuffled away. I guess he was all peopled out.

Honey set down her Snoopy lunchbox and opened it. She pulled out the red hankie. It had been washed and folded neatly into a rectangle. Maybe even ironed. She ran after Clyde and handed it to him. She must have had that hankie tucked into her lunchbox for weeks, ready to give it back.

Honey tilted her head up as he tipped his head down. The exchange between them was special in some way. Clyde gently took the hankie as if it was an injured bird that he was going to set back in its nest. They locked eyes and Clyde nodded.

And with that one small act, I got it.

Honey was scared of most grown-ups. But she saw that Clyde was a good person. Honey and Clyde probably knew more about friendship than I did. We don't always need lots of words or chit-chat.

Sometimes friendship is beyond words.

Chapter Twenty Four

Honey and I sat on the back porch, eating a paper plate filled with snickerdoodle cookies and watching Jack put a reflector on his ten-speed.

"What should we do about the camera?" I asked. "We're going to need one to get a picture of that lynx."

"I've got an idea!" Honey said.

"What?" I asked.

"Just ask your dad for the camera." She licked the crumbs from her fingers.

"Yeah, right," I said. "It cost like a million dollars. He'd never trust me with it. *Never ever.*"

"Still," Honey said through another mouthful of cookie. "You should just ask."

She was right. We needed more help. All we'd had to do was ask Clyde about the lynx, and we found out all kinds of things. Maybe asking Dad for the camera would work too.

I imagined what it would be like to find the lynx. I chewed slowly and focused on the image in my mind. I saw myself standing in Dad's den, showing my new baby sister the photograph of the lynx, in a frame that was twice the size of the others. In my mind, Dad and Mom smiled down at me proudly for being such a great big sister—and a great photographer.

But I needed a camera first, so I practiced my puppy-dog eyes to win Dad over with my charm.

Honey laughed.

Jack laughed, too. "You look more scared than sweet." Jack chucked a screwdriver into his toolbox. "Besides, I had to wait until I was twelve to use Dad's camera."

"Girls mature faster than boys," I said, repeating what Aunt Doreen had told me. Then I stuck my tongue out at him. "I'm no good at charm. I'll just come right out and ask for the camera."

Inside the house, Luke, Mark, and Matthew were on the living room floor watching Mister Roger's Neighborhood. Mom sat with her feet on the couch, her eyes closed. I was glad because I would get Dad all to myself. Honey and I snuck silently into the den.

Dad sat at his desk, whistling as he gently brushed a camera lens with a soft cloth.

"Dad," I started. "I'd like to borrow your camera."

He stopped brushing and looked at me. "*My*

camera?"

I plowed ahead before I chickened out. "There's a photo I'd like to get. It's in the woods. It's in nature. And you're going to really like it. And before you say *no,* think about what an opportunity this is. Your *only* daughter, following in your photography footsteps. Well, at least I'll be your only daughter for a few more days. Actually, you'd better loan it to me quick. You know, because you'll probably want the camera back to take pictures of my little sister."

I braced myself for his *no*. But Dad smiled at me. I was shocked.

"Celie," he said. "How about this. Tomorrow morning—early—we can go into the woods, and I'll show you how to use my camera."

"REALLY?" My eyes were probably bulging out of my head. I quickly batted my eyelids a few times to charm him before he changed his mind. "Can Honey come?"

"Sure," he said. "But remember, *early*. We leave here at 5:15 a.m. I'll explain all about natural light. And how to frame a good picture."

"Can Honey sleep over?" I asked quickly while he was in a good mood. "You know, so we can be sure to get an early start. We can have our clothes ready and make sandwiches tonight."

"Sure." He chuckled before going back to his polishing.

Honey and I rushed out to Limbo Creek Court.

"I can't believe that worked!" I hugged myself to try and hold onto the excitement.

"But is your dad going to look for the lynx with us?" Honey asked.

"Looking for the lynx is our secret," I said. "But he'll be so amazed by my picture-taking skills and care for his photography equipment that he'll loan his camera to me all the time!"

We walked in silence to Honey's house, giving me time to think.

"Or maybe not," I added, coming back down to earth a bit.

Chapter Twenty Five

As we strode up Honey's driveway, we planned what we'd say to her mother. I wasn't sure how Honey's mother would feel about a sleepover.

"We've got to make sure she's in the right mood," Honey said.

"How can you tell?"

"I'll show you." Honey squeezed into the narrow place between their garage and the fence. Brown beer bottles were lined up against the side of the garage, just out of her mother's sight.

"What are those for?" I asked.

"I'm saving them." Honey tiptoed around back and peered into the trash bin. "It'll be okay," she said. "She's on three. One beer isn't enough. Five beers is too many. Things are best when it's between two and four."

Honey was right. Mrs. Brooks seemed relieved when we asked. She stood with her rubber-gloved hands on her hips, a dirty scarf wrapped around her head. "Just don't come banging into the house at six in the morning!" she warned as she turned and finished scrubbing the counter.

"We won't!" I said.

We grabbed Honey's toothbrush and pajamas.

As we were leaving, I heard the *FWAP* of the fridge and the *FZZZT* of a bottle opening. Then a *CLINK* as the bottle cap hit the sink.

I turned to see Mrs. Brooks leaning against the kitchen counter, head tipped back, chugging a bottle of beer. She hadn't even bothered to take off her purple rubber gloves.

Chapter Twenty Six

That night as I made sandwiches, I asked a hundred questions about Dad's camera. He answered every one.

"How do you know what button to push?" I asked, thinking about the fancy camera and all those buttons and dials.

"You'll learn." Dad filled our canteens. "It's kind of like riding a bike. It might be hard the first few times, but eventually, you zip down the road without any training wheels."

"I wish I had a bike," Honey said.

"Do you always know which pictures will turn out?" I asked, thinking about the way the film hides inside the camera—sometimes for weeks—before it gets developed into pictures.

"No," Dad said. "Sometimes you're surprised. Sometimes you think you've got nothing. But when you develop the pictures, there's a surprise."

"What do you mean?"

"Sometimes you're so focused on one thing that you don't see another thing that's right in front of you. But the camera does."

I thought about that while Honey and I brushed our teeth. I wondered if I was missing something that was right in front of me all along. Something Clyde had said tickled my brain. Something about the lynx. I tried to sort it out as we put on our pajamas.

I laid out a sleeping bag for Honey. My little brothers kept bugging us so we locked the door. I opened the window and Honey and I stood together and looked toward the woods. Then, with the crickets chirping in the background, we told stories.

I told Honey what I knew about Frogtown. "There was a family who stayed in Cabin Six, in the deepest part of Wampus Woods. And in the middle of the night, someone knocked on the door. The youngest daughter, Winnie, opened the door. But no one was there. So, she went back to bed. Then someone knocked at the door again and she went to open the door again. But no one was there again. Later that night, a madman came and killed them and buried the bodies and no one ever saw them again. Now the cabin is haunted by the ghost of Wailing Winnie."

"Whoa," Honey said. "But how do you even know what happened if no one ever saw them again?"

"I don't know how I know, but it's true! Jack told me."

"Maybe the family packed up and went back to Omaha in the middle of the night," she said.

It seemed to me that Honey had shown up in the middle of the night here on Limbo Creek Court. "Your turn Honey. Tell me a story."

"Oh." Honey sat down and picked at the edge of the sleeping bag. "I don't have any stories."

"You must have at least one story," I said. "Everyone has at least one story."

I waited, listening to the rhythm of the crickets. Waiting was not something I was particularly good at.

"I have a story about peanut butter sandwiches, I guess." Honey paused. "But you have to promise not to tell."

"I promise," I answered.

"Well," Honey began. "I was about six. And we lived in Omaha. Mother had started another daycare, and she had six kids and me sitting around the kitchen table waiting for lunch. She was making peanut butter sandwiches. The first to get his sandwich was a kid named Jeffrey. He whined about the crust. So, Mother grabbed the paper plate, cut off the crust, and handed it back." Honey stopped and rubbed the edge of her pillowcase against her cheek like Matthew used to do with his baby blanket.

"That's not a story," I said. "A story has to have a

point."

"Then she cut off the crust for the other kids." Honey blinked and blew out a big breath. "I was last and I was excited. She had never cut the crust off my sandwich before. I wanted to bite into that white, soft bread with no crust. But when she turned from the counter and handed me the paper plate, all I got was a pile of crusts from six peanut butter sandwiches." Honey stopped and looked down. "Mother doesn't love me. That's the point of the story."

I would never think about crickets the same. The steady chirping had become part of Honey's story.

My mom never cut the crust off any sandwiches, but I knew she loved me. "Whoa," I whispered.

Because for once I didn't know what else to say.

Chapter Twenty Seven

The next morning, I woke to the birds twittering. I sneaked into the kitchen to cut the crust off the sandwiches I had made. I wanted Honey to know that someone cared.

Mom walked in while I was cutting. "Celie, you're wasting bread."

"But this is for Honey," I said.

"Honey doesn't like crust?"

I had promised Honey I wouldn't tell, so I said, "I don't know. But crust is hard. And Honey's life is hard enough without some dumb old crust."

Mom smiled and got out a sharper knife. "Let me do that. Go get ready."

Honey still slept. She clutched my Baby-Cries-A-Lot doll, which was much nicer than her sad-looking doll with the green marker on its cheek. She was snuggled so nicely that I didn't want to wake her up.

Spending the day with Dad was going to be great! He was going to show me how to take pictures. And how to use his fancy camera. Maybe he would develop my picture of the lynx and put it on the wall in his den—right next to Jack's picture. I couldn't wait to go! I yanked on my jeans and turned to see Honey's eyes open.

"This is a real nice doll," she said.

"I don't play with dolls anymore." I pulled out my favorite tie-dyed t-shirt. "I'm saving that doll for my baby sister."

"Where did you get it?" Honey gently combed the doll's curly blonde hair with her fingers.

"Aunt Doreen gave it to me when I was little."

"I wish I had an Aunt Doreen," Honey said.

I choked a little. Aunt Doreen was someone I didn't want to share. "Wishing for stuff doesn't always work," I said.

She dressed and we grabbed our stuff and went to the kitchen. Dad sipped coffee and dug his fork into a pile of cinnamon toast sticks made from the leftover crust. "You'd better get breakfast," he said. "The light will be perfect in an hour and we have a lot of ground to cover."

I worried that Mom would put a pile of cinnamon-toast-crust-sticks in front of Honey and I looked at Mom all panicked. But she set out two plates piled with waffles—a few extra on Honey's plate.

Honey dug in and finished her waffles and half of mine. I couldn't figure out where that skinny girl put all that food.

"We'll walk to Pitzel's Loaf & Bait and hike into the woods to catch the morning light," Dad said heading out the door.

"Do you take the picture toward the light?" I asked as we left Limbo Creek Court and turned down County Road 2.

"Not necessarily." Dad smiled as the three of us strolled in a row down the gravel. "I like to look for my subject first."

The first step is to choose your subject. I remembered that from *McGill's Guide to Wildlife Photography*. Thinking about the lynx, I worried it might not stay still long enough. "Could your subject be a wild animal?"

"It could be anything." Dad looked at me curiously.

"And you press the button and take the picture?" I asked.

"Well." Dad scratched his head. "Then you think about the frame—the other things that will be in the background."

"And *then* you press the button and take the picture?" I asked.

Miss Geagle's car zipped by us, swinging wide, and I wondered where she was going before daybreak. She didn't fish.

"Slow down, Celie," Dad said. "We'll go over all the steps once we get into the woods."

I kept asking questions while Honey trailed along swinging her Snoopy lunchbox.

Once we were close to Pitzel's Loaf & Bait, I could see bunches of cars. Probably anglers. Pitzel's opened at five o'clock so people could get their minnows early.

But as we got closer, I saw people gathered in a group outside the store. About five or six grown-ups and a few kids stood by the picnic table. People don't fish in large groups like that unless it's a fishing contest. Or maybe Gerty and Midge were having some kind of a sale on donuts. Or maybe something bad happened. Like maybe Rat Hurley shot the lynx.

Dad walked right up to a group of people at the picnic table. As he did, the others in the parking lot scuttled over to the picnic table, too. Honey and I were squished by all the folks. Miss Geagle was there with a jelly donut and a clipboard.

"Gather around class," Dad said. I looked from one kid to another as the grown-ups stood back and sipped their coffee. "Thanks for coming out so early. This is my daughter, Celie. And her friend, Honey." Some of the grown-ups smiled and said hello. "They're going to join us on our photography class field trip."

My heart popped like the tire of a monster truck driving over a rusty old nail.

Field trip? I thought this outing was just for me! Me and Dad. But I was just a tag-along on Dad's class field trip!

Tears started to well up and I quickly looked down.

"This is *literally* going to be the wildest field trip ever!" I turned to see Junior standing behind me. I couldn't help but notice the new belt buckle holding up his Toughskin jeans. It wasn't quite as big as Rat's, but almost.

"Great," I said. "Just great." Getting away from Junior was like trying to scrape a wad of gum off your shoe.

"It's no big deal." Honey moved closer to me.

But this was a big deal. Wanting a day with Dad but having to share him with half the town was almost as bad as Honey's mother giving her crusty old crust.

Chapter Twenty Eight

The sleepy grown-ups sipped coffee from Styrofoam cups. Some had puffy eyes and looked as grumpy as I felt.

How could Dad do this? This day was supposed to be great. He'd teach me how to use his fancy camera and then I'd go into the woods and get a picture of the lynx. He'd put it on his wall and he'd brag to his friends about what a great photographer I was and how I was the only one in town to get a picture of the rare wildcat.

Honey stood at my side. She leaned in, as if to hold me up, our bare arms touching. It was the only thing that kept me from crying.

The grown-ups shuffled away, slamming car doors, starting engines. Except for Miss Geagle, who waved her clipboard. "Don't mind me," she said. "Just taking notes for the summer school newsletter."

Dad smiled at the kids in his class.

"The light is perfect. Let's quickly go over the fundamentals that we've already learned." Aperture. Shutter. Frame.

I couldn't focus because I was so hurt.

When the droning about camera basics was over, Dad turned and led us down a narrow path into the woods. He showed us how to take pictures of forest plants and white pine trees. We followed him like an army of ants marching single-file toward a few crumbs to take back to our nest. Honey and I plodded along at the back of the line.

Ten minutes later, I held Dad's camera for about a total of one minute, aimed at a fern. It wasn't anything special. Dad set the kids loose to take more pictures before they headed back to Pitzel's Loaf & Bait. Honey and I turned to go.

"Wait, Celie." Dad walked down the trail to us. He strapped his fancy camera around my neck. "Now that you know the basics, go ahead and take some shots while I make sure all the kids have their rides."

"Really?" I stared down at the camera and then looked at Dad's eyes to make sure this wasn't a joke.

"Yes, Celie. Just slow down and be careful. You don't need to rush. Meet me at Pitzel's in half an hour."

I turned quickly before he could change his mind.

"Celie," Dad said.

"Yeah?" My heart sank, thinking he might ask for the camera back.

"Don't go too far." He gave me a warning look then tilted his head down to my feet. "And tie your shoe," he added before turning to go.

Honey and I rushed down a trail. I wrapped my arms around the camera, babying it just as carefully as Honey babied her Snoopy lunchbox.

"Where are we going, Celie?" Honey shouted from behind.

I didn't answer right away because my heart beat like the rumble before an earthquake. I had a camera! I needed to get close to the lynx. And I only had half an hour to find it. I hurried faster on the trail. "Let's go to Clyde's. He might have more clues. And maybe if we hurry, we can find the lynx and take a picture."

"Or we could take pictures of all the colors in his garden."

"But you know that the film is black and white, right?" I watched the tree branches overhead, thinking about wildcats.

"I can imagine the colors," Honey sang. "*Vivid Violet. Magic Magenta. Pale Pink!*"

We found Clyde in his garden.

Honey whispered this time. "*Vivid Violet. Magic Magenta. Pale Pink.*" Because this was a quiet place. A magical dreamlike place. A place where people didn't shout.

"Those are some interesting colors." Clyde pulled a scraggly weed.

"Can we take pictures of your garden?" Honey asked, still in a dreamlike whisper.

"Suit yourself." Clyde moved along a row and gently checked the stem of a black-eyed Susan.

Honey pointed to a yellow flower. "This one is my favorite."

"You'd better hurry then," Clyde said.

"Why?" Honey asked.

"Because that's an evening primrose. It blooms each night after sunset. It'll close up again before noon."

"What's this one called?" asked Honey pointing to another yellow flower.

"It's a daylily. Each flower only lasts about a day before it withers."

My time was withering worse than any flower. I had to find that lynx and get Dad's camera back to him before the primrose closed up. I blurted, "Have you seen the lynx?"

Clyde looked startled, like I had broken the spell of that magical place. He shook his head slowly. "I haven't. There's one close by." He eyed the camera around my neck. "But you're not going to find it today."

"Why not?" I asked.

"The lynx is nocturnal . . . kind of like the evening primrose."

"It only comes out at night?" I asked. "But somebody spotted one. It said so in the Farmer's Forum."

"Mostly nocturnal." Clyde stood and lifted a bucket of weeds. "And with all the bustle in the woods today, that lynx is likely to stay hidden. They don't like people all that much. Can't really blame them."

Nocturnal. That was a problem. How was I going to get out at night? And would I even want to go into the woods at night? The dark woods with all its creepy sounds sent shivers through me.

"Is the lynx dangerous?" I followed Clyde through the flowery garden trails.

"Depends on who's asking." He studied me. "Lynx like to ambush their prey."

"What are prey?" Honey asked.

"Prey are what they feed on. If you're a snowshoe hare, lynx are dangerous," Clyde said.

I bent to take a picture of an evening primrose, its three-leaf petals still fresh and sunny. But I could already sense the shift and knew the flower would soon shrivel.

We meandered through the rows of violet, magenta, and pink flowers, our conversation fading like the evening primrose.

My hopes of finding the lynx were wilting away.

We'd have to find a way to sneak out at night.

Chapter Twenty Nine

Honey and I dashed away from Clyde's place. If I showed I was responsible and got back to Pitzel's on time, Dad might let me borrow the camera again.

Up ahead, branches rustled on the trail and we stopped. My heart beat like crazy, as we listened to the rustling and waited for something to pounce. If I was scared of the woods during the day, how would I ever go into the woods at night?

Suddenly Junior was flying out of the bushes shouting. "Celie!"

I pushed past him, angry at him for scaring me.

"Guess what?" Junior jogged after me.

"What?" I rushed down the trail.

"The Farmer's Forum is having a photo contest. For the fourth of July. They're gonna publish the best picture on the front page!"

"How do you know all that?" I stopped and looked at Junior. He wiped the sweat off his forehead with his shirt.

"Your dad told us," he said. "Just now at Pitzel's."

I felt like I'd been punched.

"Listen, Celie, I've been thinking—" Junior started.

"That's nice," I spat. I was hurt Dad hadn't told me about the contest.

"C'mon, Celie." Junior took a deep breath and rubbed his hair. He looked around and stroked his *Aquamarine* camera strap. "I've been thinking. There might be a whole lot of kids looking for the lynx."

"Why?" I started walking again.

"Because it's supposed to be a nature shot. The lynx is the biggest nature story around here." He hustled after me. "So anyway. I've been thinking we should join forces. Find the lynx together."

"Together?" I asked. He sounded like he meant it. But then all my feelings bubbled up. The way Junior stopped hanging around with me at school. The way he hung around Rat Hurley. The way he and his stupid photography class were swiping Dad's time. "I'll think about it."

I had to get away from that picklehead, so I ran. Honey followed me all the way to Pitzel's Loaf & Bait. I rushed from the trees, into the parking lot, and then everything . . . everything happened in slow motion.

Dad at the picnic table, waiting.

His head slowly looking up at me.

Then down at my feet, his eyes wide.

The rustling of birch leaves.

The rotten-fishy smell as I ran past the garbage dumpster.

The tug on my foot as I stepped on my shoelace.

And my body hurtling.

Hurtling forward.

My sneakers scraping across the gravel.

Dad slowly standing.

His arms reaching toward me.

My own arms wrapping around the camera.

And Dad catching me just before I hit the ground.

But the camera still swung from its strap, hitting the gravel with a sharp, metal and plasticky ping. The shutter whirred and snapped a picture.

Time stood completely still for a second before I looked up to see Dad's disappointed face.

Dad chewed me out for being careless. After some angry words, he said more quietly, "You need to slow down, Celie. Slow down and think. You're always in a rush." He shook his head, took the banged-up camera into his hands, and walked home alone.

Honey and I sat on the picnic bench for a while, thinking about the worst morning of my life. Or maybe the second worst. A few tears tried to slip out, but I stopped them just in time.

I ruined my day with Dad. I gashed his camera so

bad, it might not work again. Even if he fixed it, he would never let me use it again. And on top of all that, Clyde said the lynx was nocturnal, so we'd probably never, ever get a picture of it.

I crossed my arms and dropped my head. "You might get your wish, Honey."

"A farm and a horse?" Her eyes opened wide, surprised.

"No," I said. I wasn't sure what she was talking about. "You said you hope we never find the lynx."

"But *you* still want to find the lynx, right?" Honey asked.

"I'm not sure," I said. "This summer is fizzling."

Without a word, Junior finally came out of the woods and sat next to us.

"But we've been having so much fun and—" Honey began.

"Fun?" I looked at her like she was crazy.

"The woods. The colors. The adventures." Honey looked at the sky kind of dreamy-like and swung her skinny legs from the bench.

"The field trip. The nocturnal lynx. The broken camera." I slumped back against the table and looked at my shoes, the one untied shoelace dangling on the ground.

"Look!" Honey pointed. Three wild turkeys pecked at the road across from the parking lot. "*Tawny Brown*. And *Blush Red* on their necks. And *Iridescent Green*!"

I had always thought turkeys were just plain brown. But I paused and tried to see all the colors that Honey saw. I pretended my hands were a camera lens and framed the birds, trying to get the light and dark and contrast just right. Honey and Junior waited while I flipped on an imaginary flash and snapped an imaginary picture. Then the turkeys scuttled behind a black spruce tree.

"If we don't find the lynx, Rat might keep looking," Junior said, looking down kind of guilty.

The three of us sat quietly on the picnic bench. Swinging our legs and breathing in and out in one big shared sigh.

"And," Junior's voice cracked. "He might shoot it with that BB gun."

Part 5:
SHUTTER SPEED

"For animals in the wild, you have to be quick. A fast shutter speed creates a shorter exposure. The shorter exposure allows the film to capture a single moment, freezing the motion of even the swiftest animal."

—McGill's Guide to Wildlife Photography

Chapter Thirty

Honey and I left Junior at Pitzel's and walked toward home.

"How are we going to get a picture in the dark?" Honey asked.

"With a flash bulb," I said.

"What's that?" she asked.

"It's like a tiny flashlight that sits on top of the camera. It flashes the minute you snap a picture, so you can see the lynx."

"But how will we find the lynx if the flash only comes on for a second?"

My shoulders drooped. "I haven't figured out that part yet."

"Let's sleep outside!" Honey jumped up and down, super excited. "And get a picture of the lynx at night."

I stopped walking. It would be scary. But that might just be the best idea ever. "As long as we're in a tent and not in a tree." Sleeping outside would mean my brothers couldn't bug us.

"It'll be a perfect night for cat food." Honey pulled a bag of kibble out of her pocket.

"We can get better snacks than that!" I wondered what went on in that crummy house of hers that she had to steal cat food to eat.

"For the lynx," she said.

"Oh," I looked at Honey. And for once I slowed down enough to really look. Dad's words were stinging in my ears about how I always rush about, not thinking. So, I thought about Honey and that cat food. And I saw something I hadn't noticed earlier. There were red marks on the side of her neck. Scratches. Scratches that looked too big for Nice Kitty.

Honey's hand shot up to cover her neck.

I got the chills along with a sickly feeling in my belly. "Honey, where's your dad?"

"He drives truck," she said. "When he gets enough money, we're going to buy a farm. Maybe by next summer I'll get a horse."

I looked at Honey's stained t-shirt, patched shorts, and sockless feet stuck in those old tap shoes. I thought about her crabby mom in that crummy house.

No one believed Honey would ever get a farm or a horse. In fact, maybe by next summer, Honey Brooks would be extinct.

Just like the Canadian lynx.

Chapter Thirty One

It was easy for us to get Honey's mother to agree to another sleepover. She barely looked up from the TV when we asked.

But my parents were mad about the camera.

"Celie." Mom dug through a kitchen drawer, jingling spare keys, rusty nails, and sunglasses. She found an old baby bottle and handed it to Dad. "You have to learn to be more responsible."

"I'll try harder." I held my breath and waited. "Can Honey ple-ee-ee-ease sleep over?"

"Celie." Dad set the baby bottle in the sink and squatted down so our eyes met. "You were careless with my camera. I'm disappointed. And I might not get it fixed in time to take pictures of the new baby."

"And with the new baby around," Mom set another baby bottle down with a clunk, "you'll have to set an example."

"I'm sorry," I said. "But I was so excited about taking pictures." They still looked mad so I opened my eyes wide and tried to look sad. "Honey's mom isn't feeling so hot. Can Honey please sleep over?"

"It's no big deal." Honey walked over to look at the baby bottles lining the counter. "Mother will be fine tomorrow. She just feels crummy at night."

Mom and Dad both glanced at Honey. Then they looked at each other. It was a secret grown-up look kids aren't supposed to understand.

And suddenly my parents were glad to have Honey over.

They even agreed to let us sleep outside. Dad helped us get the tent out of the garage, while Mom made a few phone calls. We searched for the perfect flat spot and found it between the swing set and the sandbox.

Even though Dad helped with the tent, he still didn't look happy. "Dad?"

"Hmmm?" he asked.

I took a deep breath before I spoke. "Are you still mad?"

He walked over and hugged me. "I'm just disappointed," he said. "I'll get over it."

"If you're not too disappointed . . ." Tears pooled in my eyes, so I blinked fast. "Can I ask more questions about photography?"

"Sure," he said making an effort to smile. "Ask away."

"How do you take action shots?" I thought about the lynx but didn't mention it because I didn't want Dad to get any more upset.

"Mine is the first camera with a lightning-fast shutter speed," Dad said.

"Whoa," Honey and I said together.

"One-thousand DTL." Dad paused and looked at the sky and smiled like he was just as proud of his camera as he was of his kids. Well . . . the kids that hadn't disappointed him. "What's DTL?" I asked before I thought too much about being a disappointment.

"Well, in the old days, you had to stand really still when you got your picture taken. Because the shutter speed was so slow. Now, with one thousand DTL—that means Dual Through the Lens—the shutter speed is one-one-thousandth of a second."

"That sounds fast!" Honey said.

We unrolled our sleeping bags and then followed Dad to the house for snacks. But on our way back to the tent, Junior Greyhawk's mom pulled up in her big ole' brown station wagon. Mrs. Greyhawk got out with a bag of marshmallows and some hotdog buns and headed in to talk to Mom.

As we unzipped the tent to crawl inside, we heard Junior.

"This is *literally* going to be the wildest night

ever!" he said. I couldn't help but notice the aviator sunglasses. Just like Rat's.

"What's he doing here?" I asked.

Honey shrugged.

Junior went behind his mom's car, opened the trunk, and pulled out another tent.

"Yay!" My brothers burst out of the back door. "Mom said we could sleep out in a tent, too!" shouted Luke on his way to slap Junior on the back and help him with the tent.

"Great," I said. "Just great."

"It's no big deal," said Honey.

But this was a big deal.

Junior walked over to me. "So, Celie, have you thought about joining forces?"

What I thought about was a whole list of adjectives to let loose at him. Puky. Stinky. Crooked. But Honey said, "That way we'd have a camera, Celie."

She had a point.

"On one condition," I said.

"Sure." Junior smiled and waited.

"We're not joining forces with Rat Hurley."

Junior looked shocked and even a little scared. The only good thing about this day was that at least we hadn't seen Rat.

"Sure." Junior shrugged, not too thrilled. "All right."

"We don't want a picture of a dead lynx," I said.

Junior moped away to play kick the can with my brothers, while Honey and I sat on the swings. I wondered why Junior was being friendly again. Maybe I should give him a chance. But before I could think too much, howls started far off in the distance.

Honey and I scrambled into our tent. The howls sounded like a whole pack of timber wolves. They were probably even more shaggy and robust than a lynx. I felt a tiny pinprick of fear—not for me, but for the lynx.

As the howling got louder, Honey and I scooted our sleeping bags to the middle of our tent. We huddled together, not wanting to be near the tent's walls, just in case the wolves got hungry and chomped right through.

I thought about running inside to get Dad, but then the howling changed. As if one of the wolves was horribly wounded. The howling swelled into a high-pitched screech. Suddenly it sounded like the wolf was underwater, gurgling and gasping for air. My mind was a mess trying to make sense of what was going on outside the tent.

Then the howls were mixed with something else. Laughter.

I rushed to unzip the tent. As I ran out of the tent, I bumped into Junior and my brothers who were bent over with laughter.

"You didn't scare us!" I was about to yell some real

bad words, but something rustled in the woods. We all looked toward the trees, too scared to move.

"The lynx?" Honey whispered.

"It might be a bear," Jack said quietly.

"We should go in the house," I said. Not because I was scared, but I knew my brothers weren't quite as fast as me.

Leaves rustled and twigs crackled.

A heavy stomp.

A dogwood bush trembled like it was scared.

And out stepped Rat Hurley.

He sauntered up to us and slapped Junior's arm so hard that he almost fell. "Mosquito," Rat said. "You've got to keep on top of those nasty buggers."

After that, Rat hung around Junior and my brothers.

The boys put on white sheets like ghosts and chased us through the yard.

We squirted them with the hose.

They shook our tent, jerking us awake at about three in the morning.

We got back at them by opening their tent to let the mosquitos in.

We didn't have time to watch for the lynx. The lynx was probably smart enough to stay away anyhow. By the time the birds chirped us out of a dazed sleep, our tent sagged like a wet sheet because the boys had pulled out our stakes.

We struggled with the drooping canvas and crawled out—right into a pile of Fluffy's dog doo-doo. Honey choked and I screamed, as we ran for the hose.

The boys didn't come out of their tent. But on the webbing of a metal-framed lawn chair, sitting all alone, was Junior's camera.

I quickly tucked it into my backpack.

Chapter Thirty Two

We hid in my room, peeking out the window until Junior went home and my brothers left for Jack's baseball game.

But later that morning, outside Pitzel's Loaf & Bait, Honey and I ran into Junior and Rat. My heart beat real fast. Junior kicked the pop machine and I wondered when he was going to figure out that he wouldn't get any free RC Cola.

Rat turned to Junior. "You need to decide whose side you're on Le-NERD."

A little part of me was hoping that Junior would ditch Rat and come with us. I waited to see what Junior would say, but he studied the tires on his bike like they were super interesting.

Honey and I backed away and went inside Pitzel's Loaf & Bait, where it felt safe.

"I've still got my lucky quarter," Honey said.

"What's lucky about it?"

"It's from 1958," she said.

"So?"

"It's the year they started making *Bittersweet*." She set her lunchbox down on the counter. "A kind of pinkish-orange. And my second favorite color."

"You don't need to spend your lucky quarter," I said. Honey seemed to have so much less than me.

She didn't seem upset though. And she opened her Snoopy lunchbox and dug around. Suddenly a salamander slithered right out of that lunchbox and onto the counter.

Gerty shrieked. The shriek blew out of her like she was a train blasting through town at midnight. Her eyes bulged out and her entire body shook in some kind of weird dance with her hands flailing all around and her feet shuffling away from the salamander.

Laughter exploded from outside as the boys ran away. They must have stuck the critter in the lunchbox while we were sleeping.

Honey gently picked up the salamander and carried it to the door. She let it loose in the grass under the picnic table.

The tricks from the sleepover didn't end there. Later, we stopped along Cameron Bridge Road to have a drink of water. But the boys had gotten to our canteen. It was full of vinegar. We turned on a horse trail to find a lunch spot but got lost. We figured the boys must have turned the wooden arrows to point the wrong way.

Then there was the grease on our binoculars, the POP-POP-POP of the BB gun that nearly scared us right out of our shoes, and the bug spray. The bug spray was the worst, because the boys had mixed it with something sweet, like maple syrup.

We were attracting bugs like cake at a picnic.

Chapter Thirty Three

We found our way back to Cameron Bridge Road and trudged toward the bridge, slapping flies and gnats and mosquitos. The creek was low, so Honey and I slid down the bank. We dipped our feet in the water, washing off the maple syrup bug spray.

After a while, Rat and Junior showed up. Rat leaned against the iron trestles on the bridge and laughed, the BB gun resting over his shoulder. Junior wouldn't look at me.

"You girls give up yet?" Rat shouted down at us.

"Girls don't give up!" I shouted back.

"Come on, Le-NERD," said Rat. "Let's go to Pitzel's and get some jerky."

At least they were so busy playing tricks on us that they forgot all about Junior's camera. But having that camera wasn't helping us find the lynx. My heart pumped and my brain buzzed wondering where to look next. All the advice from Clyde and Gerty was jumbled in my head.

I thought of the note with the loopy handwriting. And about the crispy ten-dollar bill stuck between the pages of *McGill's Guide to Wildlife Photography*. Maybe I should use that ten dollars to buy lynx bait, so we could be one step ahead of Rat. "We have to find that lynx before Rat finds it with his BB gun."

I watched the water tumble over the rocks. My Aunt Doreen always told me that when you didn't know which route to take, trust your gut and take action.

I shoved my wet feet into my tennis shoes and jumped up, scrambling up the bank.

"Wait, Celie!" said Honey. "What are we going to do?"

"Follow me!" I ran toward Pitzel's Loaf & Bait, Honey right behind me. "We've got to stop those boys from getting to the lynx." I *would* stop those boys. No matter what.

When we reached the edge of the parking lot, our shoes skidded against the crushed stones, stirring up a puff of dust. Sheriff Greyhawk's truck was parked in front.

"What now?" Honey asked.

"I'm not sure." I scanned the area. Junior's bicycle leaned against the pop machine, so I knew the boys were still in the store. I glanced over to the picnic table and there was my answer.

Lying on the bench, was Rat's BB gun. I knew that Gerty would never let him carry the gun into the store. But I was surprised that he would leave the gun at the picnic table for anyone to find.

"Look in the window and let me know if they're coming out of the store!" I shouted. But Honey stood with her mouth open as I rushed over and grabbed the gun and darted over to the sheriff's truck. I laid the gun behind the tire at the back of the truck, so the wooden handle would break when the sheriff backed up.

I sped away from the truck and ducked behind the dumpster, motioning for Honey to come, too.

The door of Pitzel's Loaf & Bait jingled. Sheriff Greyhawk walked out of the store with his usual cup of coffee and a hotdog. The sheriff climbed in his truck and shut his door.

As we turned to run, the gravel crunched under the sheriff's tires. We heard a loud satisfying CRACK when the wooden handle of Rat's gun snapped in two.

Chapter Thirty Four

Honey and I dodged into the woods. We paused among trees as tall as skyscrapers.

I rushed toward the biggest tree and tipped my head back. "I know where we can hide."

"Whoa!" Honey stared up at the towering white pine. She set her lunchbox down and piled pine needles on top to hide it. "I've never climbed a tree."

"This tree looks easy." I pointed to the thick branches, close together, starting near the ground. "Just follow me. And put your feet where I put mine. You'll be fine."

I grabbed the first branch and swung my left foot, boosting myself up quickly. "And don't look down until we're at the top," I warned, hoisting myself up to the next branch. I waited for Honey to catch up. Branch after branch, we climbed higher and higher.

Things on the ground got smaller and smaller, like the miniature trees and roads on Jack's train set. We stopped when the branches got too thin to hold our weight. My arms and legs tingled and shook from the climb. A breeze blew against my sweaty forehead.

We could see Pitzel's Loaf & Bait and part of Cameron Bridge Road. Being this high was a thrill! Just like the snap of Rat's BB gun beneath Sheriff Greyhawk's tire. My heart pounded remembering that CRACK!

"I'm a bird!" Honey smiled and scanned the fields to the south, the treetops, the wispy clouds in the sky.

"Just don't try to fly," I said. The tree swayed, making me dizzy. My belly fluttered as the pine needles poked into my skin and the leaves of the neighboring trees rustled. I shifted my backpack. *McGill's Guide to Wildlife Photography* weighed me down and jolted me off balance. I steadied myself and gripped the branch in front of me.

McGill's Guide said that it was good to change your perspective. Change your view. I was like an eagle, perched in the highest tree looking down at the action below. And Rat, like a tiny little ant, scurried around Pitzel's parking lot, with no idea we were watching. My heart raced with fright and excitement all at once.

"Maybe Rat doesn't know it was us," Honey said.

"Or maybe . . ." I started to feel that wobbly feeling as the tree swayed and I clutched tighter. "He's planning revenge."

"What's revenge?" Honey asked as her tap shoe slipped, crackling bark. The shoe and bits of bark went tumbling down, down, down until they landed softly on the thick pine needles below. Honey clung to the trunk, her face squished tight against the sappy pine.

Rat stopped pacing the parking lot and peered into the trees where the shoe had dropped.

"That means payback," I whispered. "We messed up Rat's BB gun and now he might come mess up something of ours."

Honey stared down at her bare foot. "I don't have much that Rat can mess up."

I felt a thickness in my throat as I studied Honey. The pine needles and branches and leaves seemed to be still for a minute as I took a deep breath and that fluttery feeling in my belly came back, but this time it had nothing to do with the tree swaying.

Honey turned her head toward Pitzel's Loaf & Bait.

Rat held his broken gun, one piece in each hand, and kicked the ground in anger. Junior walked out of Pitzel's with that happy, bouncy walk and no idea that Rat's gun had snapped. Yelling something we couldn't hear, Rat shoved Junior hard and he fell back and hit the gravel. Rat turned and hiked toward home, shaking his head.

Junior got up slowly, wiped the gravel from his hands and his jeans, and wandered, head down, in the same direction as Rat. But Junior turned suddenly and squeezed through the open gates of Blessed Sacrament Cemetery. My heart gave a lurch.

Honey and I struggled down the tree, bark scraping against our skin. I coached her down until we dangled on the lowest branch. It reminded me of the time Junior played with me on the monkey bars and I chipped my bottom tooth. I couldn't stop thinking about Junior.

But it was dinner time and a trip to the cemetery would have to wait.

Chapter Thirty Five

The next morning, it sprinkled as I walked out to meet Honey by the mailbox. The clouds continued to sputter as we walked to Pitzel's Loaf & Bait. Halfway there, the sky turned purply and the rain pelted us—like we were being punished for all the bad stuff we'd done. I didn't feel bad about Rat's gun, but Junior's camera was real heavy in my backpack.

I felt bad about all that had happened between Junior and me.

We rushed into Pitzel's just before the hail started. Outside the glass door, chunks of hail hit the parking lot, bouncing back like ping-pong balls.

Gerty peered at us over her reading glasses. I wondered if she knew about the BB gun, but I was smart enough not to ask.

"Hi, Gerty." I tried to sound real casual. "Have you

seen Junior or Rat today?"

"Junior was here hours ago. Up with the anglers," Gerty said. "He got some worms and four candy bars. He paid for the worms. He didn't pay for the candy bars."

Junior never stole anything when he and I were friends. I wondered if Rat was making him steal.

"You can take a message to those boys," said Gerty. "I've been keeping track. They owe me six dollars and forty-three cents. Those kids need more candy like a cow needs a hamburger."

Honey and I wandered around the store, waiting for the rain to stop. Honey picked out four Pixy Stix and I paid for them with the last coins in my pocket.

When the rain slowed to a drizzle, we hiked north, sucking on the Pixy Stix. Honey pointed to a trail of M&Ms, the green and yellow and red melting away across the dirt.

The M&Ms stopped at Cameron Bridge. The creek was higher than usual, swollen from the rain.

"You think he ran out of candy?" Honey asked.

I searched around. "I don't know. Maybe he jumped in the creek."

Honey leaned toward Cameron Bridge and looked into the water. I inched closer. When Honey stepped forward, I grabbed her arm and pulled her back.

"Or maybe he went up to Clyde's," I suggested.

"Or into the cemetery," Honey whispered.

We turned toward the cemetery gates. I imagined the eyes of escaped wildcats staring down at me, along with Wailing Winnie and the ghost of Lucky Lindstrom.

I figured we'd check Clyde's place first.

The path was muddy and my sneakers soaked through. Honey took off her tap shoes and buckled them together onto the handle of her Snoopy lunchbox. Then she happily splashed through the puddles.

I was too worried to splash. Worried about Rat and Junior getting back at me. About Junior stealing from Gerty. About Junior's camera hidden at the bottom of my backpack. About Junior going into Blessed Sacrament Cemetery.

Darwin bounded down the dirt lane to meet us. He went straight to Honey, who reached into her pocket and gave him a mushy piece of cookie. Then Darwin loped alongside us until we reached Clyde's shack.

Clyde appeared from a trail with a pole and a string of fish. He nodded and motioned us over to a grove under the trees, protected from the rain. He sat at a makeshift table and placed the fish on top. We watched him fillet the fish, starting with the head and carefully slicing away the skin and bones. The watery fish blood ran across the wood and dripped onto the ground. He piled the fillets on one side of the board and the scraps on the other side—the fish heads, skin, and guts.

"Would a lynx eat fish?" I asked Clyde.

"I suppose they would," Clyde said.

"Would they eat those scraps?" I asked.

"Probably. They're carnivores." He paused and added, "meat-eaters," like we didn't understand.

I shuddered, feeling the chill from my damp clothes. "I thought you said they ate snowshoe hare?"

"Right," he said. "A lynx would only show up around these parts if there was a bumper crop of hare."

"Is there a bumper crop?" I asked.

"No," Clyde answered. "That's what's so strange."

Honey asked, "It's eating something else?"

"Probably," Clyde said.

"Is the lynx sitting out in the rain getting wet?" I asked.

Those green eyes sparkled a bit as he chuckled quietly. "You know, in a lot of ways, animals are smarter than people."

"So, it's not sitting out in the rain," I said as I pulled my windbreaker tighter around my body.

"I think that lynx is tucked in some warm and cozy spot. Away from people. Away from curious kids tramping through the woods. Away from the rain." He glanced at Honey, whose teeth chattered. "You girls should follow suit."

"But where could a lynx find a cozy spot around here?" I asked. "You told us they don't dig dens."

"They don't," he said, stepping over to a bucket to wash his hands. "They might use fallen trees, stumps, existing structures. Something left behind. They're smart that way."

Honey opened her lunchbox and took out an empty beer bottle and handed it to Clyde.

I thought about how Honey said she didn't have much that Rat and Junior could mess up. Even though she didn't have much, she still found something to give to Clyde.

He gave her a sad sort of smile and nodded a thank you.

Honey shrugged. "I can get lots more."

Clyde searched her eyes for a second or two and then nodded again.

Chapter Thirty Six

Honey and I left Clyde as the sun poked out of the clouds. We followed a horse trail to a clearing and sucked on our last two soggy Pixy Stix. Honey told me about all the colors she could see. *Tumbleweed. Desert Sand. Mountain Meadow.* Her eyes brightened with every color.

I admired that. And I was glad that she was my friend.

We stepped out of the woods onto Cameron Bridge Road, creeping up to the gates of Blessed Sacrament Cemetery. Other than crossing Cameron Bridge, it was the one place in Wampus Woods that we hadn't dared to go. I checked my backpack to make sure I still had that holy water.

Honey pointed to an M&M near the gate. She crouched near the squashed candy, studying the bloody red of the M&M as it washed into the dirt.

"Should we go in?" Honey asked.

"I don't know," I said.

"It might be Junior," Honey said. "He might need our help."

"Or it could be a trap."

We tiptoed to the rusty gate, peering inside. Junior's pink banana seat bicycle was propped against a large pot of dead flowers. But no sign of Junior. And that was when I knew we would have to go into Blessed Sacrament Cemetery.

We squeezed in through a big gap and onto a narrow, two-track dirt lane. The sun didn't reach this cramped space. Mossy gravestones stuck up out of the ground, slightly crooked. I rubbed my arms and shuddered.

The grave markers near us were old—1898, 1912, 1935. But on the other side, they were newer. And that's where, in front of a shiny white gravestone, sat Junior Greyhawk.

I walked slowly to him, Honey behind me.

"What are *you* doing here?" he asked angrily.

"What are *you* doing here?" I asked back.

"What is *she* doing here?" He pointed to Honey.

But Honey was quiet.

Then I saw the words carved into the gravestone.

Pvt 1st Class Vincent "Buddy" Greyhawk
Beloved Son and Brother
March 1, 1950 – June 19, 1969

I changed the subject, which is what you do when things get awkward. Something I learned from Aunt Doreen. But I latched onto the word *brother* without thinking. "I've got four brothers. They're not *Beloved*. I'm hoping for a sister this time around. I don't need any more brothers." I chit-chatted away like I was the narrator on some boring documentary.

Junior stared at me. He stared at me hard. He clenched his fists.

"At least you have a brother!" He spat out the words, then took a few breaths. "My brother died. And what does my mom do? She moves us to her stupid hometown so we can be closer to his grave!"

Suddenly I was shaking. I didn't know Junior had a brother. I looked back at the gravestone. It felt as if I was in a dream—a horrible, sad dream. The leaves shivered and rain dripped down onto the damp, mossy ground. I wanted to run away, but then I heard Aunt Doreen's voice in my head.

I knew what I had to do.

"What happened to your brother?" I whispered.

"He *died*!" Junior said. But his voice came out weaker with a crackle at the end, and I figured my chit-chat was working.

"How did he die?" I asked, softly.

"He went into the army."

Junior was running out of steam. When he didn't say anything, I whispered, "Did he get shot?"

"No!" he shouted. And then his voice got quieter. "That's the stupid part. He didn't even die in the war or anything. He wasn't even in battle. He didn't get shot."

I waited.

"Stupid!" he shouted.

"What's stupid?" I asked.

"The way he died." Junior's voice cracked again. He slumped over and I sat down in the grass next to him.

"He was stationed in Germany. He and his buddies stopped at a pop machine. They put the money in. Nothing came out. They shook the machine. Tried to get the pop out. They shook it so hard that it tipped over." Junior bowed his head and took another deep breath. "Right onto Buddy. His head hit the sidewalk and just like that he was dead. *Dead!*"

There was so much hurt in Junior's red eyes and suddenly everything made sense. The way Junior was so quiet and whiny when he first moved here. The way he looked up to Rat Hurley, like an older brother. The way he always kicked the pop machine at Pitzel's Loaf & Bait.

Junior stared straight ahead. I followed his gaze and we both stared at Buddy Greyhawk's grave. We breathed in and out. Time stood still.

"I'm sorry," I whispered.

"And my mom made me leave stuff behind. Like my bike. Now all I got is my cousin's stupid pink bicycle." He ripped a bunch of grass out of the ground and tossed it.

"I'm sorry," I whispered again. "I know it's hard."

"How do you know?" Junior buried his head in his hands.

"Because," I said. "It was hard when Aunt Doreen died."

Chapter Thirty Seven

I sat cross-legged in the damp grass in Blessed Sacrament Cemetery with Honey and Junior. And listened to the birds. And watched the leaves sway in the breeze. And felt the dew soak through my jeans.

And I remembered. I remembered until it hurt.

Aunt Doreen skipped into the backyard for my tenth birthday party wearing a funny straw hat, big and wide-rimmed. Flowers—daisies and Black-eyed Susans—weaved in and out of the band. She hugged me with her bare, browned arms. "I need to feel the sun on my shoulders," she said.

She sat down in a lawn chair and pulled me into her lap, the metal parts of the chair creaking. The embroidered flowers on her jeans felt scratchy against my bare legs. I leaned in to give her a kiss, her cheeks sticky with suntan lotion, the kind that smells like coconut.

"Here's your present." She tilted her head and looked at me close, handing me a crisp ten-dollar bill with the note on the baby blue stationery paper. "Save it for something special."

"Like ice cream?" I asked.

She laughed. It started with a tinkly giggle, shaking her body up and down. Then the laugh burst out of her mouth, throwing her head back and her mouth so wide open I could see all the fillings in the back. I loved that laugh.

I remembered how, just two hundred and twenty-nine days after I turned ten, everything changed.

Aunt Doreen always took me to *Ellie Mae's Ice Cream Emporium* on March 1st, the day it opened for the season. Just me. No brothers. No Mom. No Dad. We would sample all eighteen flavors. Then we would sit at a table and eat three scoops if I wanted. I planned to see how *Magic Mint, Strawberry Swirl*, and *Rocky Road* would taste together. On a sugar cone, since that was Aunt Doreen's favorite, too. It didn't matter that there were still patches of ice in the grass. "A tradition is a tradition," Aunt Doreen said.

I was ready right after school, sitting on the cold front steps and watching the road. I had a surprise for her. The ten-dollar bill she gave me for my birthday, was tucked in my pocket. Mom and Dad couldn't believe I kept that ten dollars for more than a week. Money usually slipped through my hands like raindrops during a sun shower. But today I would treat Aunt Doreen. Not only a triple-decker cone but maybe stop at Pitzel's Loaf & Bait for a day-old donut on our way into town.

Aunt Doreen was coming all the way from St. Paul. After I'd waited about ten minutes, the phone rang. I heard Mom's slippers pad softly toward the kitchen. It must be Aunt Doreen calling to say she'd be late, but when a car flew toward Limbo Creek Court. I stood and waved.

As the crunching gravel came closer, my heart beat faster and I felt excited deep in my stomach. But the car whizzed by and off to the west. And as the final wisps of road dust settled down, I settled down, too, and ran my fingers along the rough surface of the cement steps, still cool to the touch. I tugged at my hat—decorated with a paisley band and a long feather, because I knew it would make Aunt Doreen laugh.

I could still hear the soft rumble of the passing car when I heard a sound inside the house. Mom gasped for air. Like she just had the wind knocked out of her. An awful sound, like when you fall hard off a swing, but don't have enough air in your lungs to cry. Then the front door banged open and Mom tumbled out, her body puddling next to me, her arms hugging me tight as she gasped and cried.

Through Mom's chokes and sputters I heard that Aunt Doreen's car had slipped on an icy patch on her way back from some protest. Something to do with saving wildlife. Birds. Clean water. Habitat. Slipped right off a bridge and into the water. Aunt Doreen died.

Everything became blurry after that.

Mom made us go to school the Monday after Aunt Doreen died. As usual, the bus picked up the farm kids first, then the up-north kids. Next, the bus came to Limbo Creek Court. Junior was last to get on, living right near town. I always saved a seat for him. But on this day, my brother Jack slid into the seat next to me, right up front by the driver. He slid close, so our shoulders touched and I leaned into him, holding back tears.

When Junior got on the bus, he stopped. I didn't look at his face, but his shoes hesitated for a second before shuffling to the back of the bus. And to Rat Hurley.

I didn't meet Junior at the monkey bars either. It was too hard to explain things after that.

Now, as I sat with Honey and Junior in the wet grass, I tried to stop the tears, but I couldn't.

I was the one that hadn't been a good friend, not Junior.

After a while, Honey said, "I guess I got it pretty good."

I turned to her and blinked, but I caught a movement in the trees. It was just a flick of fur, like when a house cat stares out a window and shudders at a bird in the front yard. Junior and Honey followed my gaze. Tucked behind a fallen birch tree at the edge of the cemetery, sitting very still, watching over us, sat a Canadian lynx.

Honey's breath caught. Junior gasped. My heart thrummed and buzzed and I felt wild and scared and . . . a feeling so big I could barely hold it in.

I marveled at the black tufts spiking from the tips of its ears. At the wide feet and powerful legs. The thick, ghostly white fur with just a touch of blue.

"*Moonbeams,*" Honey whispered.

A loon called from far away and the ears of the lynx twitched. Then everything was still and silent again.

I thought of snapping a picture, but this moment was too big for photographs. The shining yellow eyes of the lynx looked right into mine and I remembered Gerty's legend and how the lynx knew your secrets.

I thought about Honey's secrets, and Junior's secrets, and my secrets.

Maybe the lynx knew all along.

After a few quiet minutes, the beautiful wildcat turned. We watched the flashes of *Moonbeams* disappear through the trees without a sound. The only sign that the lynx was ever there was the shaking leaves of the birch tree.

Chapter Thirty Eight

Honey, Junior, and I left the cemetery and strolled on a twisty trail. The sun sparkled on us through the leaves and pine needles. The woods smelled fresh after the rain. The drooping and dripping leaves seemed to give up after a long battle.

I felt good about telling Junior and Honey my secrets. It was as if my own cloud had lifted and I breathed in the clean woody scent around me.

Honey's voice broke into my thoughts. "This day feels like *Sepia*."

"What do you mean?" Junior asked.

"It's a reddish-brown color," she said.

I looked around. "But everything around us is green."

"Sometimes I just feel colors," Honey said. "Colors are sometimes easier than words."

We sat on a pile of boulders at the corner near

County Road 2. I shared my baloney sandwiches. They were two days old and kinda smashed, but Honey's eyes got wide as she cradled the crustless bread. She took a bite and chewed, the corner of her mouth turning up in a smile.

When the sandwiches were gone, Honey and I said goodbye to Junior and walked home.

"See you tomorrow, Honey." I hurried around to the backyard.

I was feeling too many feels for one day, and wanted to be with Mom. I hoped she wasn't too busy with my brothers. But as I rounded the corner of the house, I stopped dead in my tracks.

Stretched out in a lounge chair in the wet grass, with a fruity straw hat on her head, wearing stretchy red shorts, a pink shirt knotted in the front, and blue-tinted sunglasses, was Freda Geagle.

"Where have you been?" she asked. "I've got some news."

My mood changed suddenly. I wanted to talk to Mom. I needed to talk to Mom. I couldn't talk about this stuff with Freda Geagle.

Freda continued to chatter. "I've been waiting all day for you so we could bake some wild rice hotdish. It's the best hotdish for this particular occasion."

I looked up at the sky, thinking about Junior and Honey and all the advice Aunt Doreen had given me about friendship but I had been too busy to listen. And that's when the silence hit me. "Where is everybody?" I asked.

"In the house, Sweets," Freda said, peering over the top of her blue-tinted sunglasses.

I cringed because only Aunt Doreen was allowed to call me that.

"I brought games for the boys," continued Freda. "They should be busy until bedtime, so it's just you and me. You can help with the hotdish."

"I think I'll just go to my room." I had felt enough for one day and just wanted to be with my thoughts and not listen to Freda's chatter.

"When I finish the hotdish," Freda said, following me and lowering her voice to a whisper, "we can dig into this fancy box of chocolates." She pulled a white box out of her sack, wrapped like it was from a fancy downtown store.

But something was wrong. I stopped at the back door.

"Where are my parents?" I asked.

"They had to go to the city."

"Why?" I asked.

"The *baby*." She pushed past me into the kitchen. "Your mom is having a *baby*."

"Oh, the *baby*!" I jumped up and down. "I'm gonna have a *sister*!"

"You get what you get," Freda said. "But odds are in your favor." She busied herself greasing two pans for the hotdish.

"Why two?" I asked.

"One's for the Brooks family," she said.

"Are they having a baby, too?"

"No, silly. Sometimes folks just need a little something to get them by. Nothing's better than hotdish," she said. "Except chocolate."

I went to my room and sat for a while, thinking about all that had happened between me and Junior. And about whether I was being a good friend to Honey. Thinking about these things was hard, so I concentrated on shoving my stuff under the bed to make space for the crib. Even though my parents had already put it up in their room, I figured I might still convince them to move it.

A few hours later, the phone rang. I thought that night would end with chocolates. But I couldn't have been more wrong.

Freda hung up the phone and turned to us. "It's another boy!"

My brothers cheered. I froze.

I thought back to a photo in *McGill's Guide to Wildlife Photography*. A girl ran with a triple-scoop ice cream cone in her hands, but the top scoop was sliding off and the camera captured it in mid-air. The book was trying to explain that the camera had to be set to a super-fast shutter speed to freeze things in motion. But in my mind, that scoop of ice cream just went splat on the ground.

I think I would have been all right after the shock wore off. But Freda said, "Your mom and dad are overjoyed."

"What good is another boy?" I stalked off to my room.

I thought about Aunt Doreen as I looked around at my clean floor. She had told me that you have to unpack your junk and make a mess before you can straighten it out.

Now I understood she was talking about emotions, not just Barbie dolls and puzzles. So, I tried to think about all the feels I was feeling as I took the toys and books and clothes out from under my bed.

I grabbed a cardboard box from my closet and walked back to the stack of useless stuff.

My pink tutu poked out of the pile. *Sometimes it's easier to talk in colors*, Honey had said.

"*Pink*," I said out loud as I placed that tutu into the cardboard box. I wouldn't be dancing with a little sister.

"*Green*." I picked up a plastic dinosaur, but then tossed it back into the pile, knowing my brothers would want to keep it.

"*White. White. White.*" I gently placed each piece of my play tea set into the box. I wouldn't be having tea with a little sister.

I knew one thing for sure. These feelings hurt. And

the colors didn't help me feel any better.

I reached for Baby-Cries-A-Lot. I would never play dolls with a little sister.

I sat on the floor and held the doll tight. And I formed a plan.

I wouldn't pack my doll away. I would get rid of it for good. That was the only way to get rid of this hurt.

I must have fallen asleep in the pile of junk, because the next thing I knew, Dad was picking me up and setting me down in my bed. He peeled a damp puzzle piece off my face. I shifted on the bed so I didn't have to look in his eyes.

"Celie," he whispered. "I know you wanted a sister, but you're going to love your new brother. He's got dark curly hair and eyes just like yours. And when Mom comes home from the hospital, she's going to need your help."

But my whole summer had crumbled and I just couldn't talk to him. I squeezed my eyes tight, so the tears wouldn't leak out. Dad leaned in to kiss me, his touch and the scent of his Old Spice aftershave comforting me a little. The mattress wobbled as he stood up, stepped over the toys, and left the room.

I let myself cry, my sobs muffled against my pillow.

Chapter Thirty Nine

The next morning, I grabbed my backpack and the Baby-Cries-A-Lot doll I had saved for my *sister* and pushed the back door open. Like the flash of a camera, I knew what I was going to do.

Honey sat under the cottonwood where I had seen her that very first day. Except today she was eating Pixy Stix for breakfast.

"Mother's in a bad mood," she explained.

I turned toward County Road 2 and Honey followed. Baby-Cries-A-Lot gave out a sad sort of bawl, like a wailing cat.

It sprinkled on our walk to Pitzel's Loaf & Bait.

For once, I didn't talk.

Honey didn't seem to mind. She tipped her head back watching the clouds.

The clouds were *White* mixed with a *Misty Grey*. The sky shifted from *Baby Blue* to the east and *Blush*

Pink to the west. I paused just a minute to think what those colors meant to me.

Babies. Which made me think about my baby sister. I had even picked out a name for her—Dori. And I was going to give her all the advice that Aunt Doreen had given to me. I marched on, even more determined.

Gerty was picking up trash at the edge of Pitzel's parking lot. She beamed at us. "I heard congratulations are in order!"

I tried to hold my trembling lips steady, and kicked the gravel. She looked at me, startled. Then her eyes landed on the doll and stayed there.

We marched on. Midge was at the other end of the parking lot, looking up at the clouds. She swung her head our way. "Congrat—" Midge stopped and she and Gerty exchanged a look across the lot.

"Let's go," I said to Honey.

Baby-Cries-A-Lot wailed as I marched on.

Honey followed me to the edge of Cameron Bridge. My heart beat fast. But I didn't care. I came here to do something and I was going to do it. I took a deep breath and walked right to the edge and stepped up onto the railing.

I held Baby-Cries-A Lot by her left foot and flung her as hard as I could upstream. That doll bawled as she flew through the air. Her bawling came to a sudden end when her head crashed into a rock. She bounced once and then plunged into Limbo Creek.

"Why did you do that?" Honey asked.

"Because my baby sister turned out to be a baby brother."

"But that was such a nice doll." Honey's voice trailed as her eyes tracked Baby-Cries-A-Lot bobbing downstream.

"Not as nice as a sister," I said. The doll floated along until she was underneath Cameron Bridge.

I thought about Mom and Dad goo-goo-ing over the baby. Another boy.

Honey took my hand and held it tight. The warmth of her hand seemed to defrost my heart a bit. Honey tugged me down, to sit on the edge of the bridge, dangling our feet. "I'd love to have a brother or a sister," she said softly.

I squeezed her hand. With Honey next to me, being on this bridge wasn't scary at all. I mean, I wouldn't jump off and swim in the creek or anything. But sitting here next to my best friend made me feel stronger and braver.

"Let's be sisters," Honey said. Her blue eyes searched mine, all hopeful. The anger in my heart fizzled. I thought about Honey and how she needed me, but also how I needed her. And I had needed her all along.

"Well," I said as I chucked a piece of *Desert Sand* gravel into the water. "Neither one of us has much chance of getting a real sister."

We smiled at each other and I knew Honey was better than any sister. She was a real good friend. One who had been by my side the whole time. She was there when I was scared of the woods, and scared of Clyde. She was there when Dad was too busy with his students. She was there when I spilled my guts about Aunt Doreen. And she was here now, sitting by my side even though I was crabby. As only a best friend—or a sister—would.

A large water bird swept down out of the sky. Its long *Yellow-Brown* legs hung behind it awkwardly and then straightened as it landed in a shallow bit of Limbo Creek. It stood still in the *Ocean Blue* water.

"What kind of bird is that?" Honey asked.

"A blue heron," I said. It was the bird that I was named after. "Cecilia Blue LaRue," I whispered the name quietly. "When I was little, Aunt Doreen told me about my name. The blue heron helps you to know yourself." To accept your feelings, both good and bad. It gives you strength to face challenges. The blue heron tells you to follow your instincts when you are on a quest.

I watched the blue heron and the water tumbling over the rocks of Limbo Creek. All the while kicking my legs back and forth, back and forth. The water soothed me as I thought about how Honey helped me see all the wonderful colors around me.

I wondered how I might capture the wave-like movement of the water in a photograph. The camera needs to be still, but the water would keep flowing. The photo doesn't capture the movement. Or the sound. But it captures *some* spirit of the real thing.

The heron shifted onto one leg and my eyes darted away from the water and rocks back to the bird. It made me think of Clyde with his long, skinny legs and stop-sign body and all he had shared. About the lynx and how it eats snowshoe hare. How lynx are like people in some ways, needing food, water, and shelter. Shelter. Existing structures, Clyde had said.

And suddenly, it was clear to me. The movement in the woods on the last day of school when we saw Cat-Scratch Clyde. The way Darwin had gone all wild and chased us into the woods. That run-down cabin that sat on the north bank of Limbo Creek. And what Clyde had told us about lynx using existing structures and needing water.

"I know where the lynx is!" I scrambled to my feet.

"Where?" asked Honey sounding startled.

But I had no time to explain. No time to explain all the clues that Clyde had given us. All the clues that led to the *other* side of Cameron Bridge.

I had no time to explain all this because sauntering across the bridge toward us were Junior Greyhawk and Rat Hurley.

Part 6:
FOCUS & DEPTH OF FIELD

"The lens opening, or aperture, controls the area of focus. You get to choose if all subjects are in focus or a single subject is in focus with the rest of the image mysteriously blurred."

—McGill's Guide to Wildlife Photography

Chapter Forty

"Celie!" Junior shouted. "Rudy Bearstail saw the lynx this morning. Near the road to Frogtown!"

Rat slugged him in the arm. "Shut up, Le-NERD! Don't go giving away all our secrets."

"C'mon, Honey. Let's go." I tugged her over to the north side, the boys hustling after us. Honey held back, like her feet were glued to the bridge.

Junior looked at me kind of funny. "Celie," he whispered so Rat couldn't hear. "You crossed the bridge!" And then he smiled. Like he was proud of me.

"Come on, Le-NERD!" said Rat. "Stop chatting with the hens, we've got a lynx to find."

"You won't find it," I said. "It's not where you think it is."

"Oh yeah, Celie?" Rat squared his shoulders and looked down at me through his aviator sunglasses. His BB gun was slung over his shoulder, patched with silver duct tape. "Where do you think that lynx is?"

My heart raced. "I would never tell you!"

Rat gave me a shove, and as he did my backpack slid open, Junior's fancy camera strap poking out. "My camera!" shouted Junior.

"You left it out for anybody to take," I said weakly, feeling bad for taking it, especially bad because Junior was my friend.

But I still stepped back when Junior reached for the camera.

My mind flashed back to the cemetery and the moment we shared. I figured he was thinking about it, too. He took a step back and didn't reach for the camera again.

But Rat stepped closer. He was so close, I saw grease spots on his shirt. I pictured him with his mother, cackling and chomping on platters of wild game, grease dripping down their chins. He gave me another shove. The weight of my backpack tipped me off balance. I wobbled backward.

"Don't touch me!" I shouted.

"*Don't touch me*," Rat mimicked, his face all scrunched like he was smelling a dirty diaper.

I turned to Junior. "Why do you hang around this creep?"

Junior stood back, rocking in his tennis shoes. He wouldn't look me in the eye.

"*Chill out*, Celie," came Rat's smooth voice.

"You chill out, you rat!" Right away I wanted to take that back and yell something better.

"You want to take a dip in Limbo Creek?" Rat sneered.

I thought of Aunt Doreen's warning about Cameron Bridge. About how the older boys hung out there and jumped off into the water. And I wondered again whether it was the water or the boys that I should worry about. I turned to look back at the bridge. But Honey wasn't behind me. In the scuffle, I hadn't noticed her wander away, probably chasing a moth or studying a June bug.

"Where's Honey?" I asked.

"C'mon, Junior," said Rat. "This is our chance. Let's go find that lynx."

Junior turned to me, "Come with us, Celie."

I was itching to go to Frogtown. To find that lynx. To beat the boys. I knew all the clues and I knew exactly where the lynx was.

But then I remembered another one of Clyde's clues. That lynx needed a little companionship. Just like people. "Not without Honey," I said.

Junior gave me one more look before he followed Rat.

I called for Honey. The Snoopy lunchbox was lying on the edge of the bridge, with no sign of her. I had a sickly, fluttery feeling in my stomach. I turned downstream. A leaf floated on the current, bobbing past the rocks and riffles, as far as I could see before Limbo Creek turned.

And then my heart *thunked*. Baby-Cries-A-Lot was caught up in a heap of twigs and branches with the swift water rushing around her.

And hopping across the slippery rocks, working her way toward that doll, was Honey Brooks.

Chapter Forty One

"Honey!" I sprinted to the north side of Cameron Bridge, then ran along the river bank. Junior must have heard my scream because he hurried back and ran after me.

Honey worked her way over the rocks toward the doll. But she was moving toward the deeper water.

"No Honey!" I wasn't sure if she could swim, but even a good swimmer could get tugged down in those rapids. I was mad at myself for skipping those swimming lessons. But I had to help Honey. I slid down the muddy bank and leaped onto the slippery rocks, crashing and smashing my knee against a boulder. The blood gushed.

I ignored the pain and hopped rock to rock, trying to reach her.

As I crossed, the water got deeper.

Junior struggled to catch up behind me. "Wait, Celie! Stay there! I'll go." I stood in the middle of the creek, hesitating for a minute. Then I turned and kept moving toward Honey.

"Celie!" Junior shouted from the bank. "Honey!"

As Honey turned, her bare foot slipped and she fell into the rushing water. She tried to brace her fall with her hands but fell forward into the gravelly bottom. The water rushed around her. She scrambled, trying to get to her feet as the strong current pulled her farther downstream.

I teetered as Honey tumbled and bobbed, flowing along as if she were the doll.

"Get to the bank!" Junior shouted at me. I struggled out of the water and then ran along the bank after Junior, both of us yelling for Honey.

I made it to the bend in the river, where Junior stood breathing hard. Honey had latched onto the trunk of a fallen tree. She clung to the thick trunk like a baby clings to its mother. Her eyes were wide and panicked as her head dipped under the water.

"Hang on!" I screamed. I couldn't help but feel terrified—for her and for me.

But Honey turned and focused farther out in the water, where Baby-Cries-A-Lot was caught up, bobbing along with the smaller branches, as the swift current rushed around it.

I shoved my scared feelings deep down and

bear-walked with my hands and feet onto the trunk. It swayed with my weight. My backpack and the heavy camera knocked me off-balance as I tried to grab for Honey. But she slithered farther out, focused on the doll, bobbing up and down, up and down. The doll's eyes opened and closed, opened and closed.

"Hold on!" Junior shouted.

"Leave it, Honey!" I turned my head to see Junior scrambling out onto the tree trunk after me.

"Come on, Honey," shouted Junior.

"Leave the doll!" I shouted.

Finally, Honey turned, and inch by slippery inch, she made her way toward me, fighting the strong current. She struggled to keep her body from slipping under the thick tree trunk. Her legs kicked and her arms pulled.

She was close enough for me to grab onto her arm. But her skin was slippery. Honey slid under the trunk, her head dunking underwater.

I snatched her shirt and yanked.

Junior squeezed in and grabbed Honey's leg.

Together we tugged her toward shore and out of the water, sputtering and choking.

On the bank, Junior offered me his hand and pulled me up. My sneakers squelching out of the muck. I was glad he was there. I might not have been able to save Honey on my own.

Together, Junior and I hauled Honey onto the dry

grass.

I clung to her.

The three of us sat together for a long time, Honey between Junior and me.

After she caught her breath, Honey laughed, choking a bit. She held up her left hand to show us what she had.

Drenched, scratched, missing most of her clothes, and no longer crying, was Baby-Cries-A-Lot.

Chapter Forty Two

Honey, Junior, and I lay on the grassy bank. Above us, the birch leaves fluttered happily, like it was an ordinary day, not the day that I almost lost my friend. A friend who wouldn't be here anymore if it wasn't for Junior. I was glad he was by my side, too.

"It's such a nice doll," Honey said.

"No doll is that nice!" I wiped away the blood oozing from my knee.

"This one is." Honey smoothed out the doll's hair.

"You scared me to death!" I said to her. "You could have drowned!"

Baby-Cries-A-Lot let out a gurgle and Honey giggled. "But I didn't."

"Hey," said Junior. "Let's not do that again. *Literally.*"

The three of us sitting on the bank all soggy made

me think about the wet, slippery fish out of water that time that Junior and I went ice fishing. Those fish wriggling on top of the ice, trying desperately to get back into the water.

Honey probably wouldn't have tried something so crazy if she didn't have such a crummy home.

I thought about the day we talked about a house that doesn't feel like home. And the difference between home and habitat.

I thought about the lynx's habitat then, and wondered if it was struggling to find a safe place, too.

We faced the south side of the creek, looking at its muddy bank. I spotted the place where Honey and I had landed the day Darwin chased us into the woods. The place where Honey and I stared across the bank at something white with just a hint of blue through the shaking leaves. Those shaking leaves were in the woods, just downstream, on the same side of the creek where we were now. *Right now.*

I heard a rustle and looked up to see the blue heron sweep down into another pool of water nearby. Like it was following us.

We were near Frogtown. An *existing structure*, Clyde had said.

Rat would be scouring Frogtown by now, searching for that lynx.

I had to find it before Rat did.

If I found the lynx and got a picture, we'd win the

dare. Rat would stop looking. The lynx would be safe.

"Follow me!" I crawled up the grassy bank.

Honey clutched the doll and followed, but Junior shouted, "Hold on! We can rest a while, Celie."

"No, we can't!" I shouted over my shoulder, pulling Junior's camera out of my soggy backpack and strapping it around my neck. "We have to get to the lynx first!"

"Hey!" Junior said. "My camera's all wet!"

I paused and turned to Junior. "I'm sorry, Junior. But can you trust me? I know exactly where the lynx has been hiding."

Junior nodded and I turned and walked, slowly this time, with my friends at my side, Junior squishing loudly in his sneakers.

We came out onto an old road, two parallel tracks carved into the dirt, where cars trekked years ago. Deep in Wampus Woods.

We slowed to read the signs.

FROGTOWN

Family Cabins

Weekly Rates

Kitchenettes

There were more old signs. Nailed to trees, leaning against trunks, lying on the ground.

Rock Climbing

Canoes

Nature Trails

Honey leaned down to let Baby-Cries-A-Lot smell the pinkish-white petals of a flower next to a sign that said, *Modern Amenities*. I didn't know what amenities were, but there was nothing modern about this place.

Frogtown appeared, looking more like a ghost town than a resort. I shivered in my wet clothes.

We passed the lodge and the pile of lumber that used to be Cabin One. We swatted away spider webs that blocked our path. We passed another mound of rubble. Cabin Two. The road curved closer to the creek where dragonflies danced just above the water. Deer flies buzzed around us as we crept along the road. Another pile of timber and rock gave just a hint of Cabin Three.

"How much further, Celie?" Honey whispered.

"Shhhhh." I turned to see Honey, wide-eyed. Junior breathed heavily and peered up at the trees.

We crept past an old outhouse, one wall still standing. I might have imagined it, but I was sure I smelled the musty stink from the gaping wood hole and I wondered if an outhouse counted as a Modern Amenity. A narrow trail weaved past the outhouse to another pile of wood. Cabin Five.

We padded down the road.

"Where is the lynx?" asked Honey.

"Cabin Six," I whispered.

"Why do you think that?" Junior knotted his forehead like it hurt.

I turned to Honey. "Shadows in the woods. Snapping branches. Flashes of whitish-grey with just a touch of blue."

Honey's eyes widened. *"Moonbeam Blue."*

I put my hand over her mouth. "Shhhhhh!"

I ducked to the left and tiptoed along a trail that gently sloped to Limbo Creek.

We paused, standing side by side. Down the hill, Cabin Six was all sagging wood and weathered green paint. A rope swing twisted from a tall pine, swaying slightly, as if its rider had just jumped off. The ghost of Wailing Winnie passed through my thoughts and goosebumps prickled my skin.

We took it all in, standing silently for a few minutes.

Then from under a broken plank in the cabin, half-hidden by a fallen tree, crept a lynx.

My breath caught.

"Look," Junior whispered.

"Whoa," Honey breathed.

My heart beat faster.

Honey grabbed my arm.

The lynx slinked silently toward the water's edge and I realized I was holding my breath. Then it stopped and looked up at me. It stared into my eyes for what seemed like three or four minutes. Like it could see right through me.

The lynx tilted its head to the side, thinking, the

same way Aunt Doreen used to do. I could have sworn it even smiled. Like it knew a secret.

Junior nudged me and eyed the camera strapped around my neck. I slowly unlatched the case. The tufted ears of the lynx twitched before creeping to the edge of the water.

I lifted the camera and pointed it toward the lynx and Limbo Creek. I pressed a button and the camera gave a sickly whir.

The lynx's head came up.

I didn't know if the picture worked, but I didn't have the chance to take another before the lynx leaped into the woods without a sound.

Then out from the broken plank in Cabin Six, following her into the woods, crept three small kittens.

Chapter Forty Three

Honey, Junior, and I skipped along the shady lane from Frogtown.

"That was far out!" Junior smiled at me like we never stopped being friends.

"It was *Moonbeam Blue*." Honey squeezed Baby-Cries-A-Lot.

"Is that a real color?" I asked.

"No." Honey smiled. "But it should be."

"How did you put it all together, Celie?" Junior asked.

I shrugged. "The clues were there all along. And when I was looking at the blue heron—"

"After you threw this nice doll." Honey squeezed the doll tighter and sniffed its damp hair.

I shuddered, thinking of Honey going after that doll and how stupid I was to throw it in the creek.

"And I just remembered that first day...."

Honey didn't seem to be listening and fell behind while she studied a fern, a ladybug, sap dripping from a maple tree. We stopped to wait and I turned back to Junior. "I just remembered that first day Darwin chased Honey and me into the woods."

"You were chased into the woods?" Junior asked.

"Yes," I admitted. "And we saw something move in the brush across Limbo Creek. And all the clues that Clyde gave us."

"You talked to Cat-Scratch Clyde? Are you crazy?"

"No. And he's not crazy either, Junior. You don't have to listen to Rat. Sometimes you just have to make up your own mind about people. Anyway, after I put all the clues together, I knew where the lynx was."

"Where?" asked a voice behind me.

It was Rat Hurley, stepping out from the trees. "You won't feel so brilliant when you see what's on Cameron Bridge now! Good luck, *girls*." Rat looked straight at Junior, then slunk away, down a trail, melting back into the woods like he was a woodland creature out for a little mischief.

Even with Rat's warning, Honey, Junior, and I high-fived and did a victory dance all the way to Cameron Bridge.

But that's where our victory dance ended. Standing in the middle of the bridge were two people. And even though they were still fifty feet away and a little out of focus, I knew it was Sheriff Greyhawk . . . and Dad.

My heart sank.

Dad leaned over the railing, still in his pajama pants. He was looking into the water, his hair rumpled, his arms flailing, shouting words I couldn't hear over the rushing water. Sheriff Greyhawk was on his walkie-talkie, pacing and looking away from us toward Pitzel's Loaf & Bait.

Our victory dance became a slow-motion death march toward what I was sure would be the biggest scolding we'd ever known.

As I dragged my feet through the gravel, Dad turned toward me. My heart skipped. It wasn't anger in his eyes. It was relief.

He rushed over and pulled me against his scratchy wool sweater, squeezing me tight. "Celie, you're okay," he blubbered and I felt his ragged breath turn into a sob.

Honey hid behind me, but Sheriff Greyhawk walked around me and wrapped her in a wool blanket. "Midge heard all the yelling and when we came and found that lunchbox lying there—"

"—we didn't know what to think." Dad finished the thought, shaking his head. His eyes glistened with tears.

"I'm sorry, Dad," I started. My first impulse was to blabber, "I know I shouldn't have gone in the water, but I had to save Honey."

"Of course you did," Dad said. He held me tighter, his sweater smelling like coffee and Old Spice and musty books. His unshaven cheeks scratched against my own as he brought his face down so our eyes met. His were red and extra tired. "We were so worried about you," he said.

I felt warm and cozy and squished and . . . loved. "I know, Dad." And I did know. I finally realized that he loved me all along. No matter what mistakes I made. "I just wanted to make you proud and get a picture of the lynx."

"Celie," Dad swallowed hard, tears spilling from his eyes and down his cheeks, getting stuck in his scruffy day-old beard. "I'm proud of you."

And then I saw Dad through a new lens, a clear lens, one that wasn't scratchy and blurry. The love in his face was clear.

I turned and looked for Honey. Sheriff Greyhawk helped her into his truck. Then he put his arm on Junior's shoulder and rumpled his damp hair. Junior smiled but ducked away from his touch, climbing into the truck next to Honey.

As the sheriff walked around to the driver's side, Honey and Junior turned to look my way, their faces framed in the truck's back window. Honey squeezed Baby-Cries-A-Lot and had a terrified look on her face.

I would see this image of her for days, clutching

the doll and glancing back at me. It seemed so unfair that I got pulled into a warm hug, and she got dumped into the passenger seat of the sheriff's truck, desperately clutching to that soggy old doll.

Junior waved at me and held his hand against the window.

It was then that I realized how lucky I really was. And I knew I had to be a better friend to Honey. "What's going to happen to Honey?" I asked Dad.

"The sheriff will take her home to her mom," he said as he leaned against the bridge.

I leaned against Dad and remembered some advice from Aunt Doreen. Sometimes friends need to do something hard, she said. Like tell their friend they have crud in their teeth or their deodorant isn't working. It might seem hurtful at first, but a true friend would tell just the same.

The gravel crunched, as the sheriff drove away.

I knew what I had to say and I knew it would be okay. "Dad, there's something I've got to tell you."

And I told him about Honey and her mother and that crummy house. About the beer bottles and bruises. Even about the peanut butter sandwich crust. Dad nodded his understanding as he listened to the whole story. He didn't talk at all. Just listened.

Dad pulled off his sweater and wrapped it around me. We watched as the blue heron flapped its wings and flew low over the bridge, then far away.

Dad guided me to his car, tucking me into the back seat. He carefully took the camera strap from around my neck and opened the soggy camera case.

I thought about my wet backpack and how *McGill's Guide to Wildlife Photography* was probably ruined. I'd have to tell him about that, too.

Dad studied the dials and buttons on the camera. "It should be fine once it's dried out."

Dad shut my door and walked to the middle of the bridge, bending over to pick something up. He climbed in the front seat and reached over the back seat, handing me Honey's rusty Snoopy lunchbox.

"Now, let's go home so you can meet your new brother," he said.

I wrapped my arms around Honey's lunchbox and looked out the window at the *Forest Green*, the *Sky Blue*, the *Sunshine Yellow*, and smiled.

Chapter Forty Four

Two weeks later, on my eleventh birthday, I got up late and rushed to the kitchen.

Mom cracked an egg into a gigantic bowl of cake batter. "Happy Birthday!" she said.

I pecked her on the cheek and squeezed her tight. "I'm going to meet Honey!" She was going to celebrate with me.

I ran to Honey's front steps and rang the bell. No answer. I ran around to check the backyard. Empty. The lawn was mowed and the saggy fence was fixed. Even the beer bottles on the side of the house were gone.

My shoulders slumped. I pushed the gate open and went to wait on the front steps. As I ran my hands across the cold, rough surface, I thought of the last time I waited on my own front steps for Aunt Doreen.

A sad and sore feeling rose in my stomach as I thought about losing Honey, too. I had the urge to jump up and run away, but I didn't. I sat with those feelings. The achy tingling spread from my stomach to my chest until it squeezed my heart. I sat for a good, long while and let the sadness wash over me. A fly buzzed, a dog barked in the distance, crickets chirped.

Thoughts of what might have happened to Honey squeezed into my brain. The achy tingling turned panicky and my heart thumped against my ribs. As my breathing came faster, I thought of the way *McGill's Guide* said to take deep breaths and hold yourself steady to keep the camera from shaking. I closed my eyes, took deep breaths, and thought of all the colors of that summer. My brain calmed and my body relaxed. I lost track of time.

A rumbling motor roused me, and I gazed blearily on an old red truck rattling toward Honey's house. The truck pulled into the driveway and Honey jumped out, holding her lunchbox and Baby-Cries-A-Lot. That dark feeling in my belly vanished and warmth washed over me.

"Happy Birthday, Celie!" she said.

We rushed together and hugged.

"Where were you?" I asked, pulling away and looking into her eyes. But before she could answer, a white-haired man got out of the truck. He reached for a crooked cane and whistled as he limped down to check the mailbox. "Who's that?" I whispered.

She shrugged. "My great uncle."

"You never talked about a great uncle," I said.

"I didn't know I had one."

I wanted to ask if she was mad at me for telling her secrets, but I'd worked hard on listening. I knew Honey's mother went away for a while. Mom said Mrs. Brooks needed time to heal.

Honey walked over and sat on the steps. She opened her lunchbox and pulled out a sheet of paper. "Your present," she said. It was a picture of three lynx kits, colored with a mixture of *Goldenrod* and *Lemon Yellow*, playing in the *Forest Green* grass. I smiled, remembering the way we told Junior we'd get a picture of a lynx as part of the dare.

"Uncle Anders bought me brand new crayons," she whispered.

I stroked the picture. "We're both good at drawing," I said, thinking about my lost blue-ribbon artwork from the last day of school.

"And we're both left-handed," Honey said.

"How do you know I'm left-handed? I've barely touched a pencil since school got out."

Honey dug to the bottom of the lunchbox and pulled out left-handed, green, rubber-handled scissors. The initials, C.B.L., were written on the blade with a magic marker.

"My scissors!"

Honey shrugged. "I found them on the last day. I thought somebody threw them out."

"How did you know they were mine?"

"I didn't," she said. "At least not right away."

I studied her face. Her cheeks were more freckly than when I met her. She wore a new purple tank top and mismatched lime-green shorts.

"I'm going to stay with him for a while," she said. I felt a stab in my heart. And if that wasn't enough Honey's uncle pushed something into the front lawn. With each *thwack* of his mallet against the FOR RENT sign, I felt my heart break just a little more.

"And guess what?" Honey said.

"What?"

"He has a farm . . . and a horse. It's an old horse and we can't ride him, but I feed him carrots and apples and brush his mane." Honey breathed in the fresh air and tipped her head back to smile up at the sun.

Honey was happier now and I was glad.

"Honey," I said. "Are you mad that I told about your mom?"

Honey looked out at the lawn, then tapped her *Brick Red* cowboy boots against the steps. "I was scared," she whispered.

"I'm sorry." I looked down at my own scruffy sneakers.

"It's okay." She took a deep, shaky breath, blowing out real slow. "Mother boiled over. But Sheriff

Greyhawk kept hold of her until my uncle came."

"Time to go!" Honey's uncle called.

"Aren't you coming to my party?" I asked, surprised.

She looked at me for a minute, then at her uncle. "Hold on, Celie. I'll be right back."

Honey ran over to her uncle who steadied himself between the truck and his cane. He bent down and turned his ear toward her. She said something and pointed at me. He smiled and patted her head with his bony hand, brushing her bangs away from her face. Honey hugged him tight, smashing her face into his baggy overalls before she skipped back to me.

"My uncle's going to the Farmer's Fleet store in town, so I can stay at your house until the party," Honey said, all excited.

Honey's uncle drove the old truck down Limbo Creek Court, slowing in front of Dad who stood at our mailbox. Uncle Anders and Dad exchanged a few words before the red truck pulled onto County Road 2 and puttered toward town.

I reached over and held Honey's hand. "Even though you're going away, we can still be best friends, right?"

"No." She shook her head and my heart stung. But she squeezed my hand tighter and said, "We're sisters, remember?"

My skin got all tingly and it felt like the sun rose in

my chest.

Once I stopped rushing through the bad feelings, I had time to feel—really feel—the good ones. I held that good feeling, as the morning's *Tangerine* sun brightened to *Lemon Yellow.*

Chapter Forty Five

D ad grilled hamburgers and sweet corn. Mom set up folding tables in the backyard with pretty tablecloths and streamers and balloons. Clyde even stopped by with a crate full of homemade root beer. He didn't stay though.

Junior rode up on his bike—which was now *Jade Green*. "Hey, Celie. Hey, Honey." He jumped off his bike and bounced on his toes in that same way that always made me feel happy. Junior spent the last two days helping Midge clean out fish tanks at Pitzel's Loaf & Bait, so we had plenty of bait and had been fishing once. Even if Rat hadn't been sent to Scottsdale to stay with his grandma for the rest of the summer, I knew Junior would always be my friend.

Jack walked out of the garage and helped Junior turn his bike upside down. They watched the wheels spin around and around and around. It reminded me of Gerty's hotdogs, spinning endlessly on those rollers at Pitzel's Loaf & Bait.

"What's it like to have a new baby?" Honey asked.

"He's real cute. And too small to pick on me. And Mom's smiling again now that her legs aren't swollen sausages." I explained to her about babies as we walked to the picnic table where Mom cradled Andrew in her arms and chatted with Gerty, Midge, and Freda Geagle. Freda had a newspaper—some kid from the next town over had won the photo contest with a picture of a bald eagle.

"He usually just lays there," I continued telling Honey about the baby. "And squirms. Once in a while, he cries. And that can get real loud. He goes through lots of diapers. And they can get real stinky."

I sat down and Honey squeezed between me and Mom.

After a few minutes of staring at the baby, Honey asked, "Can I hold him?"

She set down her Snoopy lunchbox and Baby-Cries-A-Lot and Mom showed her how to hold Andrew's head so it didn't flop back.

"Whoa," Honey whispered and sniffed the baby's head. "This baby is way better than any doll."

"He sure is." I ran a finger across his cheek, amazed how anything could be so soft.

"Celie, your dad has a surprise for you," Mom said.

"In the den."

I almost forgot about birthday presents! Honey carefully handed Andrew back to Mom and we hurried into the den.

Sitting on the corner of Dad's desk was *McGill's Guide to Wildlife Photography,* all tattered and wrinkly from getting wet. I opened the book and the spine cracked. I turned to page 115, with that familiar handwriting in the margins. I took out the ten-dollar bill and the crumpled note with those same loopy letters.

I turned back to the first page with the lesson on choosing your subject. The lesson I skipped because I was in a rush to read about the lynx. As I ran my finger slowly over the crinkly page, I noticed more of that loopy cursive writing. At the top of that page, it said, Property of Doreen Blue.

This had been Aunt Doreen's book! Goose bumps prickled my arms.

I set the book down and unfolded the note as Junior walked in. We read Aunt Doreen's words together: "How you spend a crispy ten-dollar bill says a lot about a person."

"I know exactly how we're going to spend this money," I said.

"Ice cream?" Honey asked.

"Yep," I said.

"Butter brickle?" Junior asked.

I nodded. "Triple deckers at *Ellie Mae's Ice Cream Emporium*!" I carefully folded the note and the ten-dollar bill in half and stuck them in my pocket.

Dad walked in and pointed to the black and white photographs lining the wall. The fish and the waterfall and the squirrel. At the end of the row, there was a new frame. But where I expected to see a lynx, was a fuzzy out-of-focus blob. I was sad the picture that I took of the lynx hadn't turned out.

"Look closely," Dad said.

Something behind the fuzziness grabbed my attention. Clear and completely in focus, framed nicely by the leaves and the trees of Wampus Woods, was a bird. A great blue heron.

I felt a chill. Dad had said when you take pictures, sometimes you focus hard on one thing and you don't see what's right in front of you. He was right.

I thought of the first time I saw the blue heron, standing on those long, skinny legs. I figured it was telling me to be brave, like when I jumped into Limbo Creek after Honey without thinking.

But now the bird had a different message. Sometimes you have to follow your instincts, but other times you have to follow your heart.

I knew we had saved Honey Brooks from more than a swollen creek.

Honey and Junior stood on either side of me and we linked arms. The three of us looked at the picture of the great blue heron for a long time.

Aunt Doreen was right about ten being the best age. This *had* been my best. *Our* best.

Me and Junior and Honey Brooks.

Acknowledgments

This story has been a long time coming and many people helped make this book! Kendra Levin provided kind words in my first workshopping of the book. Suzi Retslaff reviewed an early version. Suzy Morgan mentored me through the first revisions. Linda and Selina were my New York writing partners and provided lots of laughs during our writing sessions.

I acknowledge the help and encouragement from my past and present critique partners: Betty Raum, Linda Sand, June Dordal, Kristy Olsgaard, Deirdre Prischmann, Deb Beauchamp, Sarah Page, Kim Larson, Terrie Enlow, and Missy Jackson. And I appreciate Ms. Kelsey and her fifth graders at Middleton Elementary for all the wonderful notes and classroom visits over the years.

Finally, I thank Kiri Jorgensen and her team at Chicken Scratch Books for seeing the beauty in this story, and I thank Connie Resch for turning the words into a wonderful and inspiring cover.

About the Author

Tory Christie

Tory Christie is a scientist by day, studying rocks, water, and the environment. When she's not at work, she writes children's books about science, technology, and nature. She loves the synergy between making science topics more understandable and writing for children. Tory Christie lives with her family, a rabbit, a dog, a cat, and two frogs in Fargo, North Dakota.

Chicken Scratch Reading School
A Touch of Blue
www.chickenscratchbooks.com/courses

Join us at Chicken Scratch Reading School for your choice of 2 different online Novel Study Courses for *A Touch of Blue*. Created by certified teachers with extensive curriculum design experience, these offerings are 4 or 6-week courses of study for 4th- 8th grade students. They include reading study focus, interviews, quizzes, vocabulary work, thematic and character analysis, a written essay, and culmination project. The courses include a mix of online and on-paper work, highlighted by instructional videos from the instructors, Julie DenOuden and Kiri Jorgensen, and the author, Tory Christie.

Chicken Scratch Books creates online novel study courses for every book we publish.
Our goal is to teach our readers to appreciate strong new traditional literature.